ARKANA

The Absent Father

Alix Pirani is well known as both writer of poetry, plays and fiction, and as a practising and teaching psychotherapist. She runs creative mythology workshops, and contributes to the training of therapists within the disciplines of humanistic, neo-Reichian and transpersonal psychology. Alix Pirani has four children and lives in Bath.

ALIX PIRANI

The Absent Father

Crisis and Creativity

The Myth of Danae and Perseus
in the twentieth century

Illustrations of original paper-cuts by
ABI PIRANI

ARKANA

ARKANA

Published by the Penguin Group
27 Wrights Lane, London W8 5TZ, England
Viking Penguin Inc., 40 West 23rd Street, New York, New York 10010, USA
Penguin Books Australia Ltd, Ringwood, Victoria, Australia
Penguin Books Canada Ltd, 2801 John Street, Markham, Ontario, Canada L3R 1B4
Penguin Books (NZ) Ltd, 182–190 Wairau Road, Auckland 10, New Zealand

Penguin Books Ltd, Registered Offices: Harmondsworth, Middlesex, England

First published by Routledge 1988
Published by Arkana 1989
10 9 8 7 6 5 4 3 2 1

Library of Congress Cataloging in Publication Data
Pirani, Alix
The absent father: crisis and creativity: the myth of Danae and
Perseus in the twentieth century/by Alix Pirani: illustrations
from original paper-cuts by Abi Pirani.
p. cm
Bibliography: p.
Includes index.
1. Sex role. 2. Patriarchy—Psychological aspects.
3. Perseus (Greek mythology). 4. Danaë (Greek mythology).
5. Masculinity (Psychology). 6. Femininity (Psychology).
7. Mythology, Greek—Psychological aspects.
8. Archetype (Psychology). I. Title.
BF692.2.P57 1988 155.3'3—dc19 88–2383

ISBN 014.01.9164 X

Filmset in Sabon

Made and printed in Great Britain by
the Guernsey Press Co. Ltd.,
Guernsey, Channel Islands.

To my children
And their absent father

And in memory of my father

Contents

Contents

Section II   Myth and process

Acknowledgments

This book is the culmination of many years of therapeutic, personal and literary experience and owes much to the people I have worked with in therapy, in workshops, and in writing groups. The specific experiences of many of them are recorded here anonymously, and I am grateful to them all.

Many men of my generation are the 'absent fathers' of this work. Those who have most influenced my thinking are James Hillman, Stanley Keleman, the late Frank Lake, Peter Redgrove and D. M. Thomas. My contact with them personally and with what they have written, and the relation between the two, has taught me a great deal about absent fathering.

Younger men have, wittingly or unwittingly, been Perseus to my Danae/Medusa, and I acknowledge all they have given me. My three sons Simon, Daniel and Adam have sought and found meaning alongside me, each in his different way. I have had invaluable support from colleagues Howard Cooper, Peter Hawkins, Alan McMurtrie and, especially, John Kirti Wheway. He read and commented helpfully on an early draft of this work.

The 'absent mothers' whose theoretical writing has most inspired me are Rosemary Gordon, Liz Greene, Sylvia Brinton Perera and Marion Woodman. The women who have encouraged and supported me personally are numerous. My daughter Abi has faithfully shared many of the pains and delights of the journey, and has contributed her own striking illustrations to this volume. To Jane Malcomson I owe a great deal, for she first introduced me to the power of myth and dynamic ways of working with it, and we co-led the Absent Father workshops, which gave rise to my writing this book.

Lorna St Aubyn and the Michaelmas Trust made a generous loan to enable me to take time to pursue my explorations of women's spirituality and to write.

My debt to Barbara Somers, guide and friend, is immeasurable. Her encouragement and loving intelligence over the past years has been an unfailing resource, and our mutual trust has held me to my trust in the creative process throughout everything.

Introduction

Fathers are missing: away at work; separated by divorce from their children. Paternal authority has been eroded, yet paternalism is still in evidence, and under attack by the women's movement. The credibility of male political leaders is at a low point, the spiritual fathers are alienated, and God the Father is a fading concept.

The absence of felt fatherhood and fathering affects us at every level: in our personal lives and in our collective experiences. With the shift of power, the instability, has come a release, and a loss, of vital energy: new responsibilities for women and challenging questions for men.

Patriarchy is by no means dead. In our present need to halt its seemingly relentless progress toward global annihilation we know that only the balance between masculine and feminine values, the combined creativity of men and women, of fathers and mothers, will save us. Yet there seems to be a want of male responsibility and commitment to the task of fostering life in the family, or life on earth. Masculine power is exercised either in an inappropriately over-controlling or weakly impotent way: it is failing to be supportive and effective where it is most needed.

Each of us has an inner man and woman, masculine and feminine qualities. The relations between them, their interactions and actions, reflect and affect the collective, the balance of male and female 'out there'. And we each have an internalised family: mother, father, daughter, son. That family reflects and affects our families 'out there', and the family of humans on earth. If the supportive father abandons the family, the inner personality, the world, will the breakdown mean the end of everything? Who will survive?

The crisis is not new: only the apocalyptic scale is new. The world of the Greeks was small by our standards but not by theirs. Ancient myths contain the same stories as those we live by today; the same archetypal patterns of human behaviour. Their handling of crisis can be for us a guide, a focus for reflection on our own crises.

The story of Danae, of the birth and adventures of Perseus, is very much a story for our time. A threatened father tries to confine and control his daughter; a single mother brings up her son on her own, without the support of parents or husband, but with the protection of a would-be stepfather; the son has to cope with the absence of father, and live with the increased but still unclear power of mother: out of all this experience he must find new directions for himself. Perseus becomes a reluctant destroyer of the corrupt patriarch and an ally of the benign feminine; but he also slays the poisonous feminine, the Medusa, and from her beheaded body is born Pegasus, symbol of liberated spiritual imagination. Perseus rescues the threatened Andromeda and, marrying her, finds a new role for himself as husband and father.

At every stage this myth explores the balance of masculine and feminine, in their benign and malign aspects, and it leads to a healthy resolution. It is concerned with generational development, with blocks to creativity, with envy and the nature of destructivity. It explores the relationship between body, mind and spirit. It has particular relevance for older women, whose maturity and wisdom are too easily lost to society. Insofar as a valid guiding father is absent just now, mother's wisdom is much needed.

The myth took hold of my imagination seven years ago. Since then I have found myself living it in my personal life and sharing it with family and friends. I have worked with it with clients in therapy, in the 'Absent Father' Workshops in Creative Mythology which I co-led with my colleague Jane Malcomson, and other workshops in creativity. (These are described in chapter 13.) I have seen it playing itself out on a wider scale in generation interactions and world events. At this point in time it seems our civilisation is slowly learning how to slay its Medusa and release Pegasus, and is confronting the monster which is threatening Andromeda.

Introduction

Perseus and Andromeda had a daughter, Gorgophone. She was distinguished for being the first woman who declined to throw herself on her dead husband's funeral pyre. It seems right and eminently hopeful that the granddaughter of Danae should refuse to submit to that patriarchal rite. Woman, the feminine, must not allow herself to perish in the holocaust that marks the demise of patriarchy. 'Holocaust' means a sacrifice in which the whole victim is burnt.

Myths reflect the archetypal patterns out of which they grow: they carry questions rather than answers. The patterns are present in the mind and in the body: the myth resonates deeply with our physical experience: cellular, vegetative, muscular. The imagination engages with it; we play out its story consciously and unconsciously at an interpersonal level. And it is our individual inner drama: each of us has within us a Danae, a Perseus, a Medusa, a Pegasus, and our realisation of their story can release in us a more liberated imagination, and creative powers which challenge our too narrow view of what we are. For most myths are about evolution: the continually evolving relationship between left and right brain, old and new brain, animality and humanity, humanity and divinity.

To use – that is to re-create – the myth, hold it in one's conscious and unconscious trust, is therapeutic. To be aware of how it is working through one's feeling body, and through the body politic, accords with a homeopathic, poetic view of cultural health.

The first section of the book follows the story of the myth as it is read and lived at the everyday level of private and public awareness. In itself it inevitably leads us – as it led me in the writing – into a deeper understanding of the processes we are all part of, which I examine in the second section. In exploring there the patterns of creativity and of body-life within the myth I found myself in deeper waters, experiencing much of the sickness and anti-life, the crisis of creativity and healing, that I had somewhat glibly indicated in the title. But as the myth itself tells us, only by going into the Medusa's cave and the place where the corruption of power and energy is at its worst do we reclaim that power and use it to heal ourselves.

It may be that some readers will want to read the second section in parallel with, or before, the first, depending on their familiarity with this kind of material.

I shall be using the terms 'masculine' and 'feminine' to denote – roughly – the left-brain and right-brain aspects of our functioning, which correspond – roughly – to the Yang and Yin principles, and the animus and anima polarity. Social conditioning has produced a correlative but quite different 'male' and 'female' distinction which is largely about roles. Each man and woman is influenced by biology, custom, upbringing, to manifest these energies in his or her individual life. The use of these terms and the arguments that sometimes rage around their use and meaning is obviously part of a significant revaluation that is going on. I want to make it clear that I shall use them freely to suggest or imply certain kinds of polarity, but without any intention to harden a classification or value-judgment or fix a meaning.

I have come up against one particular problem – namely, the proliferation of material to which I might refer, both imaginative and theoretical. It would be impossible to be comprehensive, so I have restricted references to written works which have had a particular appeal to me. This is no way implies an invalidation of anything else available. There is a growing body of writing by women on spiritual issues. As for the myth, that is open to expansion, interpretation and adaptation: nobody, fortunately, has a copyright on it. Jungian psychologists have written substantially on this and other myths. The Medusa has a very large bibliography and appears repeatedly in imaginative literature; one of the earliest ancestors of horror fiction characters, her popularity rating is high. What is important is that she is seen as part of a continuing story; her dangerous power is precisely that one gets stuck with her.

Several versions of the myth exist: there are many variants and details which I have omitted. I have used mainly Robert Graves's material in the Penguin *Greek Myths*. His spare unembellished style I appreciate and recommend, for it leaves us free to exercise our own imaginative involvement and expansion.

Section I

The myth and its meanings

The myth

Acrisius, King of Argos, consulted the oracle because he had no male heir. He was told he would have no sons, but a grandson, who would kill him. He locked up his only daughter Danae in a dungeon – but Zeus came down in a shower of golden rain and impregnated her, and she bore Perseus. When her father discovered it he put her and her infant in a wooden chest, sealed it and cast them into the sea. It was ultimately washed up on the shore of Seriphos, caught in the net of a fisherman, Dictys, who released Danae and Perseus. He was too poor to look after them, but took them to his brother the King Polydectes, who received them into his house, where Perseus was now raised. Polydectes tried repeatedly, but without success, to force Danae into marrying him, and as Perseus grew to manhood he protected his mother from the King's advances. In order to get rid of Perseus, Polydectes sent him to fetch the head of the Gorgon Medusa, a creature so frightful that all who looked on her were turned to stone. The goddess Athena, who hated the Medusa and had been responsible for her horrific appearance, came to Perseus's aid in various ways and gave him a brightly polished shield so that he might see the Gorgon's head reflected in it and not face her directly. Thus Perseus was able to behead the Medusa. Out of her bleeding body sprang the winged horse Pegasus, who was to become a source of nourishment for the Muses and an occasional servant to the gods. After further adventures – including the resue of Andromeda from a sea-monster and his marriage to her – Perseus returned to Seriphos and held up the Medusa head before Polydectes, who was thereby turned to stone. Dictys took over the throne and Perseus, Danae and Andromeda set out for Argos. Acrisius tried to evade them by going to Larissa. But Perseus was invited to take part in the funeral games which the King of Larissa was holding to honour his dead father, and when he threw the discus the wind diverted its course: it struck Acrisius's foot and killed him, to the dismay of his grandson. Perseus would not take over his grandfather's throne, but established himself elsewhere as king and father of a new dynasty.

Chapter 1

Acrisius and Danae:
The crisis of fatherhood

A middle-aged divorced woman said to me, having become unexpectedly pregnant,

> 'No, I didn't take proper precautions – and you know it feels just like a teenage pregnancy. It seemed as though the whole world was telling me I mustn't love. And I was in a kind of glow of loving that made me feel real, and that mattered more than caution and responsibility. If no husband or father is there to look after me, but only to disapprove of me having this affair, I'm going to fling caution to the winds – and prove it's *my* body and *my* life . . .'

The similarity with Danae was striking: an unfeeling father figure has condemned and abandoned her; Zeus's shower of golden rain comes in a 'glow of loving'. A 'teenage pregnancy' – for a woman with teenage children of her own and a responsible job in social work. She had as much difficulty relating to the hierarchical system in which she worked as she had in relating to father and ex-husband, and spoke often of men's egotistical 'heartlessness', of her problem of maintaining and not compromising loving values.

She was only one of many women I know – friends, clients – who feel starved of love and critical of men, and I share those feelings. (Danae's name means 'She who judges. The parched one.') Unhappily married, divorced, single, because there seem to be so few men a woman of independent spirit can commit herself to, we struggle with problems of deprivation, frustrated creativity and family turbulence, yet we seem in our struggle to be trying to find

4

new meaning to 'loving': we have rejected heartless relationships and want something other than unholy matrimony. At times we spurn men wholly; at times we are drawn to them magnetically in spite of ourselves. We are constantly teased by this creature, and we reluctantly admit the truth of what he is saying: 'Man is never inside, femininity is pure, free, powerful: but man is everywhere around . . . he is in all eternity the creative absence . . . The feminine world [is] a world without men, but entirely constituted by the gaze of men.'[1] However, that gaze can have many meanings. At the moment I think it is watching us with a tentative expectancy; what is Danae going to give birth to?

A closer look at her story helps us focus on the male figure who, in reality, or imagination, or internalised in our psyche, puts us in this situation. Danae, impregnated by the golden god, was a familiar figure to male romantic artists and writers. Some feminists now refer to her as having been raped by Zeus. Both ignore the origins of her imprisonment. It is the mortal, her father Acrisius, who is the crucial male force, the initiator of the crisis and the journey that follows. It is his patriarchal decision and his abdication of fatherhood that has to be looked at. His name means 'Ill-judgment'.

The withdrawal of 'good' fatherhood

Acrisius is at first an all-too-powerful 'present' father; but his vulnerability is exposed when he and the patrilineal connection are threatened by the oracle. There will be no son, but a grandson will kill him. The king denies his destiny, tries to cheat death, and turns tyrant: the good caring father absents himself from his only child. Egotism and insecurity lead to a determination to prevent growth, kill rebellion, suppress sexuality. Readers will have no difficulty in recognising modern counterparts of this ruler and father. Beneath his actions lies great fear. Identifying with him in a workshop, one man said, 'I'm really frightened. I'm behaving like a brute, but I feel completely hollow inside. I'm losing everything. My power is a sham . . . I'm afraid of my love for her . . . I'll turn my back on her, and go and sit on my throne.'

The lonely throne symbolises well the position that any person granted power and authority is pushed into; but in all of us is

Acrisius's fear of growth, of the creative generational process itself, which involves ultimately our own personal death. Powerful men, in our society, dare not acknowledge this vulnerability: many do not know they have hearts until they have heart attacks. Inside there may be a frightened unloved little boy, but the stance of dependable paterfamilias and worldly competent male must be kept up. Everyone seems to have an investment in propping up what may be a very shaky phallic figure, starting from 'Just wait till I tell your father when he comes home' and reaching corrosively cynical proportions when powerful presidents are openly acknowledged to be incompetent façades.

Biologically a man is vulnerable at the exact point of his functioning. He is identified with the head in its many meanings, with exposed external aspects of the body. His sperm loses its head when it enters the ovum, his raison d'être is felt to disappear if his penis cannot get an erect head. He is expected to be head of the family, to use his head to get ahead. If his heart is inactive and he lacks spiritual awareness the connection between head and sex, his own fertility, is polarised and mechanical. Death may terrify him, but he can get by if his head doesn't think about it, and the stiff upper lip shows his bravado. Biologically a woman cannot remain in her head, nor avoid knowledge of growth and death. She must submit to the life-process and its rhythms, through the monthly cycle of blood-loss, through childbirth and breastfeeding.

Acrisius and Danae represent the conflict within each of us between our wish to control the life-and-death process and our willingness to go with it. The conflict has been given to men and women to play out: the crisis of creativity lies in the fact that the excessive power men are given and try to adopt is untenable. Meanwhile women, subordinated, suffer patiently. And they are wiser therefore, but ignored. 'I'm submitting to him' said one woman, acting as Danae. 'It's all I can do. But how can he be so obtuse? So pig-headed? And where's my mother?'

The absence of Danae's mother from the story marks the impotence and enfeeblement of woman's influence. Our patriarchal God has no consort. We now have either the intolerably controlling father-leader suppressing potentially rebellious women and children (or his internal woman and child), or the weak, absent father-leader who has almost no authority with his family or society (has an internally scornful woman and child).

In the family, if father is weak, the mother may manifest the autocracy of Acrisius. In society this comes out in the strident political 'new women' who behave more like domineering men than sensitive women. They deny the radical nature of the crisis. Society, like the family, like any project, is in deep trouble if there is no acceptance of the uncontrollable or unforeseen, of decay and death, as elements in its development. Acrisius's panic reaction, his narrow egotistical interpretation of the oracle's statement, can only cause more pain as he resists the inevitable.

The repression of Danae's sexuality

The myth symbolises the way a possessive father may lock up his daughter's sexuality. He binds the girl to himself: usually by a mixture of seductive caring and puritanical dominance – or a tantalising remoteness that makes her obsessed with trying to win his love: psychic if not physical incest. As a girl's sexual feelings grow in adolescence they will only be able to mature if her father honours and validates them and allows those feelings to develop. For this he needs to be clear in his own sexuality, able to accept and contain it. A perversion of fatherly love, deliberate or unaware, can trap her in a prison that makes it impossible for her to love other men.[2]

Many girls who enjoy the protective and close love of their fathers in early childhood suddenly lose it when they reach puberty. They never forget the shock of his unexpected removal from them, this unexplained absenting of himself. The same shock and bewilderment is felt by those identifying with Danae as she is locked up by her father. Menstruation is being seen as a source of shame, sex as a temptation, the growing woman therefore dangerous to father and to family stability. Beneath such attitudes lies a deep fear of the mysterious feminine, of the woman's connectedness to life and death processes, of her ability to give birth to a Perseus. The exaggeration and alienation of male power originated in that fear of woman power. The gods take over because the menstruating goddess is too threatening, unpredictable.

Danae was helpless, but many women are now turning to goddess images to help them reclaim that power which lies in their sexual-spiritual qualities – different qualities from the maternal or intellectual, which men can more easily control. Different aspects of feminine power are personified – or deified – in the myth. 'Liberated' women are having to come to terms with what their power as women really is, if it is not to be simply aped manpower. Only by granting themselves their full feminine capacities and wisdoms can they offer a valid alternative to a decaying patriarchy: the myth suggests what those are and how they are likely to be recovered. But, significantly, it is Perseus, the masculine energy, who explores and reclaims those powers.

Just as some women are essentially colluding with patriarchal modes of power, so in individual experience the daughter may collude with her father's incestuously controlling impulses – because she can't herself cope with the power and vulnerability of her own deepening and expanding sexual and heart feelings: her mother cannot cope either. She represses her own sexuality, sacrifices it, out of love or fear, to him: she needs him to keep her in a prison. One woman admitted this honestly, making a virtue out of necessity, sitting in the dungeon she'd just been put into: 'I don't mind – I'm special here – he'll be sure to visit me often, and now I've got power over him. Who cares about other men anyway?'

In the next chapter and in chapter 12 we shall see how this prison exists in a woman's body, in a way which binds and inhibits her. Many women are to some extent always married to their fathers, not their husbands, and the full creativity that could inform marriage, family and society is blocked.

Absent fathers: the missing generation

When Acrisius denies Danae a mate and creates the absence of a husband-father he is, in effect, castrating his son's generation, out of jealousy and fear of being superseded. As often happens ironically in myths, the attempt to deny the oracle almost automatically produces the predicted event. Acrisius does rob himself of a male 'heir', and so weakens the patriarchal line, the male connection.

In our own social-political sphere we see how this has happened during the last century. The authoritarian father's over-control has been reacted against to the extent that men 'don't know how to be fathers any more', as they often put it.[3] Over-permissiveness has been one extreme unfortunate reaction: in effect the autocratic father has annulled his son's strength and authority.

The tyranny of European male leaders of two world wars, and the submissive patriotism of their women, brought about mass slaughter of the younger men who might have been husbands and fathers. Wilfred Owen's 1918 poem re-telling the story of Abram and Isaac in the context of the war, ends:

> . . . an angel called him out of heaven,
> Saying . . . Offer the Ram of Pride instead of him,
> But the old man would not so, but slew his son,
> And half the seed of Europe, one by one.[4]

The loss to women has been great and the effect on children severe. There is a generation of men and women, born in the 1940s, who literally slept with their mothers in childhood, many of whom were damaged by that experience, and by the trauma of coping with the absent father's return – and in many cases he then left again for good. When the children are male their response to inadequate fathering is to fulfil the oracle: a generation of grandsons appears who are led to overthrow the old regime – as they started to do in the student movements of the 1960s. The destructiveness is inevitable. As we shall see later, Perseus (whose name means 'the destroyer') is destined to kill, almost involuntarily, the patriarchal monsters and the tyrannical patriarchs. Until this revolution in fatherhood is completed – and the myth suggests some of the crucial stages it will have to go through – we live with the absence.

The nature of men's working lives, their own alienation and identity confusion, have eroded their capacity to be fathers and to be valued. To have fought unwillingly in a disintegrating, dehumanising war, whether on a real or commercial battlefield, is not to be the hero one's family is willing to welcome back and support. A father's once-respected role as guide in the world of work and social organisation is lost when his work is meaningless and his power in society minimal, ineffectual or negative. So his family may despise him for his impotence and reject him when his frustrations turn him into a bully in the home. His capacity to be a spiritual guide is largely lost. The idealism and vision of political or humanitarian commitment may partially meet this need but it tends to be ego-bound, without true humility, because within himself he feels deeply humiliated. Many men leave home, or die young, because they have no place or authority there and are outfaced or pushed away by a wife and children who seem not to need them other than as breadwinners, or to meet their needs.

The uncertainty so many thinking people now have about the nature of fatherhood is covered up: little attention is given to it, while the media – and serious anti-sexists – make capital out of the sex war, in effect indulging in the irresponsibility of bickering parents, and avoiding the fundamental issue which is affecting our children's future. That is how we are dealing with this state of painful transition. The pain emerges in groups, when women, and men, get through their defensive rationalisations, politicising and arguing, and are able to express, perhaps through Danae, their desolateness, their fear and anger at the loss, the often gaping wound caused by the absence of a father or a husband, however bad he is, or might be. When the father's control and patronage goes, we can lose our bearings, abandoned and cast adrift on a sea of emotions, without direction, like Danae in the sea-chest.

A woman may choose to bring up a child on her own, deliberately taking the Danae path of single motherhood. To some extent it can be refreshingly free of distressing uncertainty and conflict. It leaves her having to face, however, many frightening experiences and awesome challenges which she could not have visualised. Here, as in so many real, and mythical situations, the woman, the feminine, goes, willingly or not, into the underworld, carrying the burden of lost hopefulness, to endure the life-threatening isolation, the loss of self-hood and identity which the man, the masculine, is reluctant or unable to experience.[5] Acrisius tries to avoid his own fate but leaves Danae to hers.

Chapter 2

Zeus:
Sex, spirit and divinity

Acrisius locks up Danae: Zeus, in effect, releases her. Before he appears she is helpless, imprisoned, deprived, her needs as a woman denied. She may be anything from submissive and acquiescent to rebellious and disbelieving. Behind both extremes lie a despair and hopelessness: there is seemingly no way out.

It is the despair that brings Zeus in, though he may on the face of it be attracted by the submissive or the rebellious sexuality. The powerful Zeus, like all gods, is a project of human fantasy: we fantasise to ease our suffering or our sexual need, and often the latter is exaggerated to mask the former.

In desperate straits, if we allow ourselves to feel fully the hopelessness of our predicament, seemingly trapped and without power, then we can find the way to discover the meaning of our situation and transcend it: we see it from the perspective of a god – and that is another, greater power. Zeus can 'save' us according to the spirit in which we call him up, consciously or not. We may not know at first what our need for him is; nor even that we do need him. It is Zeus who finds Danae, apparently uninvited. She is full of wonder at his arrival, can't as yet understand it. Like Danae, many women want to be liberated from stifling male domination, want greater sexual freedom and self-determination, but have yet to realise fully what is happening when they grant that to themselves, what the meaning of that freedom is.

Zeus's role in the story is crucial. His intervention in the activities of the humans must challenge our assumptions about sex, fertility and the meaning of our existence. His ambiguous symbolic status brings to the foreground our need to invent gods and myths to embody the visionary in us.[1]

The god's infiltration into the dungeon is 'as a shower of golden rain'. Whether he then takes bodily form, or Danae is simply impregnated by the shower, is not stated. So we are straightway involved in the ambivalence of the symbolism that is used to bridge the gap between the human and the divine. The golden rain suggests the blessing of the sun-god and his bounteous seed, the liquid, radiant quality of sexual energy: the 'glow of loving' spoken of by the woman quoted in the previous chapter; a beautiful image and just right to bring life and nourishment to 'the parched one'. This symbolic quality I shall explore later (chapter 11) in examining the myth as a description of creative process; meanwhile let us assume that Zeus comes to Danae in the form of a potent human male – which would accord with his general reputation. He might be seen as the roving god on the lookout for attractive girls, deciding to enjoy Danae who can't escape him. He could be responding genuinely to her distress and loneliness, her need to love and be loved. We know also that he is defying and tricking Acrisius – now we may be in a 'Lock up your daughters' comedy situation. It's worth remembering that the paradox of Zeus is a joke – Jovial.

However, the joke is a serious one. Zeus is defying man's attempts to outwit the oracle, fate, the gods, and to control growth by destructive and oppressive means. He represents the biological imperative, and is no doubt the god responsible for the persistent small percentage of contraception failures. The 'joke' of an unexpected pregnancy is always on us humans. Zeus is the god of illegitimacy, and will appear whenever what is 'legitimate' needs to be called into question – and the implication is that biology and divinity are inseparable, that there is a spiritual, a higher meaning to our biological presence on earth than we can be aware of with our limited vision. Furthermore, it is part of the phallic, the male function, to drop his seed on good earth, to inseminate, procreate. At times he will do it promiscuously, indiscriminately, unable to see where the best earth is. Yet even in this he is serving a 'higher' purpose, whether he knows it or not. The 'teenage pregnancy' is a fundamental challenge.

Zeus recognises the 'good earth' of Danae and ensures that there will indeed be a grandson to overthrow the tyrant. This purpose is benign: he is bringing humanity and divinity to replace

13

heartlessness. He creates a child the meaning of whose life is not known but will unfold in time, a son who will be called on to manifest the spirit that fathered him.

In the Absent Father· workshops the role of Zeus always presented a predicament when the group came to improvise a modern version of the myth. Men taking part had difficulty handling the role of lover-seducer-divine, and the Danaes – incarcerated, in different workshops, in a mental hospital, finishing school, convent, and reformatory – were embarrassed by the ambivalent sexual-spiritual approach of – respectively – the Jungian analyst, guru, Dutch reformed priest and pastoral coun- sellor who visited them. The pair found themselves caught in salacity, cynical flirtation, phoneyness, and felt themselves unable and inadequate to express love seriously: humour and self-mockery saw them through. One man, himself an ex-priest, expressed later his anger at having betrayed his finer self and of having been betrayed in this situation.

It was a reflection of how much awkwardness and bewilderment there is around issues of sex and love, and how easily the two are split off from each other, producing unease, guilt and mistrust in one's own motives. If we say that Zeus seduced Danae, or that she perhaps, in her damsel-in-distress helplessness, seduced him, what judgment are we putting on the word 'seduction'? Can we imagine that they were drawn to and by one another and made love in full and equal awareness of what they were doing? If we can visualise a mature sexual meeting of that kind, an act of loving, then we are implicitly taking responsible cognisance of what follows. Danae's attitude to her child will be very much influenced by the quality of this initiation. That the myth is so unspecific suggests again that conception may happen in any number of ways, but it is our conception of that conception that will affect the being that is conceived. Danae knows that she was impregnated by the god: the myth constitutes a continuing evaluation of what that divine conception generates. The father god we invent determines and is determined by the son he fathers, be it a real son or a creative work.

It is possible to see Danae's insemination as autonomous. There is a mythic tradition of 'self-impregnation', where the woman desires and values herself such that she gives birth to her new self. It goes back to the original creatrix, the archetypal self-creating earth- goddess who preceded patriarchal religion.[2] The sense is partly of

auto-eroticism, partly of a powerful virgin purity: a chastity that is a strength: fully self-affirmative. Danae maintains that integrity throughout the story.

Marion Woodman has explored this condition of pregnancy in her book *The Pregnant Virgin*, and makes a useful distinction between rape and ravishment – ravishment by the god being a symbol of that self-impregnation.[3] The point needs taking by feminists who cry rape, for if Danae can fantasise, invent Zeus as part of the self-reproduction, then we must question the need to fantasise a rapist. There is an important issue here also about masturbation fantasy, and I discuss that in chapters 11 and 12. A Danae who experiences Zeus as another violator, another Acrisius, never emerges from prison.

Zeus's relationship with Danae in fact parallels and challenges her relationship with Acrisius. Between the father and daughter there may be mutual seduction, incestuous appropriation and psychic rape. But Zeus does not control Danae, makes no claims on her. She is free, within the bounds set by her father, and is about to be liberated from them by her pregnancy. The paternalistic tied relationship is unholy and controlling, the uncommitted spontaneous relationship holy and liberating.

In the absence of a loving human husband, of peer status, these are at present the alternatives: an uncomfortable and unsatisfying situation, one that many women now live with. They reject the paternalistic heartless man and the ties associated with conventional marriage, and opt for 'inspired uncertainty' – a Zeus condition – ways of relating which in their unfamiliarity and insecurity are a considerable challenge to the courage and imagination: multiple relationships, celibacy, lesbian relationships, single motherhood – sometimes via A.I.D., the nearest we come to Zeus's visit.

Problematic as it is, this freedom is giving women a golden opportunity to re-assess their attitudes to sex and to body-life.[4] And this is being done basically in a spirit of serious quest. Every woman has a Zeus – a golden opportunist – within her, and shouldn't deny it: a need to rove, to be irresponsible sometimes, and to take a broader, higher view of mortal life and behaviour than is possible when she is buried in home, husband and children. Ideally this kind of need should be met in adolescence and young adulthood prior to a commitment to making a family. But it is rare that a young woman experiences it genuinely: the ostensible freedom often conceals a deep-rooted dependency on the father. We could say that womankind is going through an adolescent maturing process now as it breaks away from patriarchal control. Hence the older woman's 'teenage pregnancy'. In later life many women are now courageously and good-humouredly re-living the missed adolescence, with all the embarrassment, clumsiness and lack of dignity that go with that process. With luck they find men who understand and don't ridicule them.

The patriarchs imprisoned women in their homes and their bodies. Of course their biology will always 'trap' them to a certain extent: Danae must bear the baby and care for it, and will always feel the conflicts that accompany the maternal tie. But she need not lose her independence of spirit therefore. The way a woman's body-life and creativity can become stagnant is clearly portrayed later by the Medusa, a sort of closed-circuit corruption of the feminine. 'Independence of spirit' – a Zeus quality – allows sex to be experienced not as part of a power-game, a fight for conquest or control, but freely and honestly. It can then be re-connected to love and commitment, to the heart. It is a 'holiness' in which we can aim for purity without being puritanical, sanctity without being sanctimonious, and a good deal of joviality. This is possible when we take full charge of our own individual sexuality – men as well as women. First we grant ourselves the freedom to learn about its nature: then we come to accept the paradoxes inherent in it and make appropriate choices from a place of maturity.[5] This cannot be done without a revaluation of the prevailing debasement of sexuality by society through the media (a revaluation which Aids now forces on us urgently).

The paradoxes of sexuality are those which have never ceased to exercise human beings: questions of soul, incarnation, the flesh and the spirit, a body's manifestation of a life's meaning. They are awesome questions: gods were thought up to 'embody' them. Myth itself is a way of incarnating, giving form to, the puzzles implicit in being mortal and vulnerable to pain. When Danae is impregnated she enters the condition of parenthood, which always presents an acute existential challenge: what is the point of this generative process? Zeus's role here is to ensure that human beings do not stop asking that question.

It is asked by people who wonder what kind of world they are bringing children into. The myth highlights our present situation: Acrisius is the blind proud patriarch who threatens the cutting off of fertility, the annihilation of love and of future generations. He does this out of fear of destruction of his own small regime. (Many people choose not to be parents because of that fear.) Zeus is the god concerned with survival of the race: he defies us to look at what we are doing, to ask about the meaning of life. He comes unexpectedly, disguised perhaps, and we need to be open to receive him and trust the inspiration we are given.

It is Danae, the powerless one, who lets the god in. Those who strongly feel that we are in a trapped and hopeless position are met by Zeus, who inspires them with intense commitment to life – people such as Greenpeace and Greenham activists. They carry our hope for life, our desperate determination to find a way out of the prison: find the creativity needed to avoid global destruction. The male survival instinct and 'sky' spirituality is wedded to the female 'earth' fertility and concern for future generations: Zeus wedded to Danae. This simple basic inspiration is vital, no matter how much intellectual or political reasonings try to distort, complicate, control or undermine it. Acrisius, so the myth tells us, does not believe Zeus came to his daughter: he has the characteristic cynicism of politicians and intellectuals. It is Zeus's making love with humanity which we must, like Danae, trust as a source of creative power. The myth, as it continues, gives us an idea of what is likely to happen to those who carry the opportunity, the devotion, and the burden of restoring meaning and value – humanity and divinity – to life on earth. Some individuals take these 'missionary' roles of Danae and Perseus consciously, but they are meeting the needs of the collective unconscious. Every single mother and fatherless son is playing out the drama of a society in need of a new father, as surely as Mary and Jesus did.

Chapter 3

Beyond the prison of the womb:

The birth and single mothering of Perseus

Perseus is born in a prison: the image is rich and resonant, carrying all our hopes for the emergence of a new liberated life even out of the old restrictions, a life which seemingly, for a newborn, holds infinite promise.

The innocence is there without doubt, but the knowledge of the prison is there also. Danae carries it, and she and her baby are one before and after the birth. And since they only have one another they are in danger of imprisoning each other, just as they are later imprisoned in the chest that Acrisius casts on the sea. A potential shadow lies already over Perseus's future.

How does Danae's experience affect her baby? Much has been learned in recent years about intra-uterine life and the relationship of the foetus to its mother and her world, and the birth itself is a crucially conditioned and conditioning event.[1] If Danae feels depressed by her imprisonment, angry, afraid of the future, lonely, sexually deprived, then her baby feels it also. Indeed the unexpressed feelings, the 'locked up' energies, are turned inwards, conveyed to the foetus in a kind of secret communion: the baby is imprisoned in an unhappy womb. Such emotions will poison the mother's baby as surely as a poisonous diet, alcohol or nicotine. There are also of course feelings of pleasure and excitement at the expected birth, but the future, for any Danae, is very uncertain.

Equally, muscular tensions will affect the unborn baby's growth and, even more powerfully, the labour and birth experience. A woman whose sexuality has been locked up will have chronic pelvic

19

and uterine tension, and will fight rather than facilitate the birth process, however much she may consciously wish to go along with it. She tenses against this overwhelming experience as against any expression of growth which is life-threatening. This is the internalised Acrisius. The baby's experience at birth can be terrifying if mother is an imprisoning womb. It is a matter of degree: there is always trauma. The general experience, as recreated in primal regression, in LSD therapy and in dream-analysis, is of being trapped in a prison from which there seems for a long time no escape, followed by a massive struggle, invigorating or devastatingly violent, to get out. The particular individual experience imprints itself on each person's future efforts at self-assertion, self-liberation and creativity. However, the next immediate phase is crucial: if the child and mother are immediately bonded in contact, they heal each other by restoring the familiar heart-to-heart pulsation of the womb connection, sharing and resolving their distress in an exchange of love. If this doesn't happen the trauma of separation is severe for both (see Leboyer 1975).

We may suppose that Perseus has a distressing birth experience, a firstborn fighting his way out of an unhappy prison: he will carry that with him and will later confront the depressed life-threatening mother in the shape of the Medusa. But we may also assume that he is considerably healed by the immediate close contact with his mother which the myth suggests in their sea-chest journey. This must make all the difference, giving him a basic trust in woman and her ability to meet his needs and accept whatever distress or destruction he may have to cause in order to be free. His healthy relationship to the feminine in the later stages of the myth are testimony to that trust.

A newborn baby knows it has hurt its mother and needs not to be made ashamed or guilt-ridden about that. Danae in her loneliness accepts, loves and holds Perseus: he is the god's child. A woman who believes in the essential 'divinity' of her child, aware that another soul is entrusted to her care, will not basically reject him, however much his birth or subsequent struggles for self-determination may cause them both intense pain and mutual violation. The wonder and mystery of the birth of a new child calls up in us feelings of great awe: joy and hope. Blake put it well; he acknowledged also that there is no easy ride ahead:

The angel that presided o'er my birth
Said, little creature, born of joy and mirth,
Go love, without the help of anything on earth.

If we look again at the prison context, we see how it is reproduced exactly in present-day handling of childbirth. That it was ever named a 'confinement' speaks for itself. Under male-dominated obstetric practice a woman's need to experience, and learn from, the process of childbearing is suppressed by drugs, interventions and the imposition of a medical view which corresponds exactly to Acrisius's desire to control the process, to conquer death even when it is not imminent, deny any wisdom that does not belong to his established practice, and avoid experiencing his own pain or seeing Danae's. Many women in our hospitals actually have Danae's experience of being alone, closed off from contact, the baby's father absent, and an ominous dictatorial male consultant hovering in the background. Frightened, angry and helpless, their cries of pain are further stifled by drugs: the emotions and the drugs are shared by the baby. Natural rhythms and the natural way of expressing them are interfered with.

Where a mother is extremely stressed she may experience a murderous hatred of the absent or intervening people who are failing to support her: this she may well turn towards the baby itself and consciously or unconsciously wish to kill it. Even babies who are not actually battered can sense that: they inherit the impotent rage and may later act it out: violent grandsons of the authoritarian patriarchy. Suppressing a woman's destructive feelings and her free expression of them, in any sphere of life, will lead ultimately to an eruption of violence and destruction elsewhere, usually by men. The Nazis were sons of women who had been confined to Kinder, Küche, Kirche. Perseus will focus his destructiveness appropriately, but his destiny is already determined. In this way he can be seen as Danae's 'animus', in the Jungian sense. He also could be called her right arm, since his right arm will perform heroic deeds and kill the patriarchs who have oppressed her. He will be, as many sons are, his mother's expression of power in the wider world. There is a parallel here with the Genesis story from which monotheism developed. Eve, disgraced and condemned to suffer pain in childbirth by God the father, very weakly husbanded by Adam, gives birth to Cain, who becomes a murderer.

To quote from a woman in primal regression therapy who was able to re-experience aspects of her own and her son's birth:

... My own re-enacted birth was an experience of suffocation, near-dying: I had to break everything to get out: I was getting the message clearly that my father in the background, who didn't really want me, was controlling my mother's desire to give birth, and she was holding down her anger against him, and holding down my aggressive need to get born ... That conflict remained with me: I was a girl, not the son my father might have accepted – Acrisius all over again. I suppressed my assertive energy, submitted to father and later, after a shotgun marriage, to husband. When my son was born I was in a state of tremendous unspoken rage at the heartless behaviour, the lack of support, of both men, and at my mother's weakness. This was acute at the time of the actual hospital birth. It was a dreadful experience: I suffered an agony such as I'd never known before and felt so desperate and alone that when my baby arrived I could easily have killed him, I hated him so. I soon forgot all that of course. We enjoyed good contact later: he was a delight and I loved him dearly. But I know now I was holding him in, as I'd been held in: he must have had an appalling birth experience. I suffered severe post-natal depression for months. Soon after this my husband left us. My son always treated me in a rather apologetic, guilty way; but he became a fighter, a political revolutionary, and a direct violator of my conservative father's most cherished orthodoxies. He's never known his own father.

This process is inevitable: revolutionary ideas are born out of prisons, from places of frustrated anger. The women's movement has had this experience: its own internal Perseus, its animus or right arm, sometimes 'goes out on a limb' with its destructiveness. Fortunately the movement also has Danae's devoted protection of its inspired brainchild. In their individual and family lives, women need to realise and express their anger, if need be in a therapeutic setting, or in the political arena, lest it manifest itself elsewhere in their children's wanton aggressiveness. Behind so many vandals, hooligans and terrorists are mothers whose capacity for loving and creating has been firmly suppressed or frustrated.

The dark sea crossing

Acrisius, still failing to 'get the message', disowns and rejects his daughter and her child, casting them out to sea in a sealed chest. This is their most critical time, yet it is the place where they are bound to grow together and truly experience together the worst: depression, fear, hopelessness, exhaustion. This replicates the birth experience, and it certainly represents post-natal depression and the identity-loss that follows on birth for mother and child. (In the next chapter I shall look at the way this ordeal is experienced by wives and children who lose paternal support – the loss of the whole family's identity.)

Though such experiences are currently intensified for women who suffer the absence of men, they are ordeals that are fundamental to the life-cycle, to the death and rebirth of identity at different stages in the life process. Severe depressions often precede 'creative breakthrough'. What makes them so hard for us to bear in our Western world is that we lack acceptance of their inevitability and have no rituals, as more primitive societies do, to help us through these transitions.[2] When we are in 'the valley of the shadow of death' our distress and depression will be shunned, tranquillised, misread, silenced. Many are thrust into the dark sea-chest of an unenlightened mental hospital. Some go under; others survive. Faith, and a sense that there must be a meaning to the experience, will bring a person through. Danae, in this black enclosure, knows of the oracle, knows Zeus cared about her; but sometimes even that faith may be lost: the god is absent and we lose touch even with him. Locked in our darkness, directionless, we have to give up to being carried along by unpredictable fate. Yet there is an instinctive hanging on to life. Danae may ask herself why Acrisius didn't simply kill them and have done: there was a vestige of caring in him, and a giving over to a fate that might be more benign than he himself. In states of depression our own internal Acrisius puts us in a kind of hell but doesn't reject us totally. People sometimes talk of 'going on automatic pilot'.

When we come through such experiences and land on the other shore we know that there was a meaning to them. Perseus, in Seriphos, will begin to discover and re-create that meaning.

Consciously or unconsciously, humankind is experiencing this at

the moment. We are in the dark, threatened by ecological or nuclear death. Vestiges of caring are occasionally seen in our rulers, but we have no guarantee that the dangerous craft they have put us in won't sink. All we can do is trust, as Danae has to, that we may survive, to reach the safety of the other shore, and with Perseus make meaning of what has happened. We can identify with Perseus the innocent baby: he may feel some of the stress but knows nothing of the real danger. We need to acknowledge how little we know. Perseus can only be what he is – a breathing, trusting, growing newborn, undeterred from being alive. If like him we can, in each present moment, be fully alive, then the forces of death do not prevail. The signs are hopeful, for many individuals, groups and movements are riding the depression, finding a meaning to the crisis, asserting their vitality (see Rowe, 1983, 1985). Every 'single' person can, in her or his way of being in the sea-chest, affect the collective, and the support we give each other in crisis is, here and now, an assertion of our humanity; within each of us is a hopeful Perseus, a free child.

The myth itself supports us. It suggests that Danae – the woman at peril – will survive in her commitment to the child, with a woman's selfless sense of the continuity of the generations and her knowledge that as a man he will perhaps have more strength than she has to destroy, re-build, re-structure the future. This applies to the feminine and masculine qualities we each have inside us, and also to the way women may relate to the 'non-patriarchal' men who are emerging to envision and implement a new society based on bisexual power. Women must value these men.

Meanwhile it is the Danaes who are too much left to sink or swim: not only unsupported women but all the carriers of inspiration in our world: those with vision, vocation, a dedication to humanity – creative artists, educators, healers, spiritual guides. Where they are not actually persecuted they are at best sorely unsupported and subtly ridiculed. Our ancestors seemed better able to accept the existence of the unwelcome oracle, the seers or prophets. Though their messages might be threatening or subversive, their spiritual vision and wisdom was respected. But it may well be that the ordeal for today's Danaes in our society is precisely that lack of recognition, the acknowledgment that they are carrying the god's child. Acrisius feared and respected the gods, though he failed to recognise them, and tried to cheat them. Today's Acrisius doesn't believe there are any gods – other than the One who reflects his own image.

25

Chapter 4

Danae, Perseus and Polydectes:

The absent father, the shadow father, and growth

This poem was written by a woman who had chosen single motherhood; she found, when she went into the sea-chest experience, that she was more frightened than she had ever admitted to herself, and that there was much to mourn before she would feel strong enough to carry her burden:

> In this dark constriction
> I carry my son forward;
> And that other vile restriction
> Is behind me.
>
> My heart grieves
> For the father who hurt me;
> And my heart weeps
> For the god who kissed me
> And gave me this child.
>
> I want to reach forward –
> Offer it to him, show him.
> But he is back there,
> In the past from which I'm parted.
>
> I have no direction.
> Arrival is meaningless.
> There may not be another shore to reach.
> And if there is –
> He will not be standing on it.

She said of her feelings in the sea-chest:

'I seem to have lost everything that mattered, that could look after me. I have my son and I'm his mother, but am I going to be able to *be* a mother? I've no mother to help me in this.
I've not much idea how my son will grow up. Yet at first I felt so brave . . . I feel I'm doing the right thing, that I know better how to be a parent than his missing father – but I'm not all that sure.'

This conflict between feelings of weakness and strength, the insecurity of the woman conditioned to dependency when she becomes independent, is what brings many divorced and single mothers to therapy for help in coping with their lives. The new context of single mothering, of fostering a child's growth without a firm paternal presence, is increasingly commonplace and truly a transitional ordeal in which all bearings may be lost. I can describe here only some of what is commonly experienced: the more familiar it becomes, the more positively it can be lived with. The sharing of our insights, our own stories and the meanings we make of them is essential. Books such as Judith Arcana's *Every Mother's Son* and Maureen Green's *Goodbye Father*[1] are supportive and constructive in the very best sense: they see the situation as potentially creative. That is most important: the sea-chest experience, depression and mourning, are part of a vital process. Abandoned women and their families act defensively, out of their hurt and in response to social attitudes. Society tends to express shock, blaming, and then off-handed complacency, at the divorce rate and the breakdown of the family, publicly unable to cope with the loss of the old structures. Each woman, each absent father, each family has to find the meaning of the experience.

For the woman who loses the support of her husband after some years of marriage and family-rearing the effect is severe: it can rarely be visualised in advance. Even in cases of relatively little hardship she experiences an increase of power and responsibility as a parent and a loss of self-confidence and status as a person: this she may cover up with hyperactivity. Initially there may be an invigorating relief from marital tensions but then in time she may come to neglect herself as a woman, having to play father as well as mother. She may be too weak to cope, or she may become overbearingly powerful for her children, perhaps harm them with her bitterness towards the missing father, or her transferring of positive or negative attention to a favoured or disliked son or daughter. Or, aware of such dangers, she suffers anxiety that she is too strong or too weak an influence. Whichever way, she carries a heavy load and too often feels, out of a sense of guilt or pride or martyrdom, that she must carry it without help. Her guilty, angry feelings will be increased as the children vent on her, the one available parent, all the distress and anger they feel about both parents.

There is a strong sense of betrayal. The children usually carry clearly the mark of their father's absence, suffering resentment and a persistent feeling of deprivation. It affects them socially, since father usually guides and establishes his children in the 'world out there'. As a representative of that world, and an authority, his approval, encouragement and support are needed. So too is his ability to cut the cord or apron-strings that bind mother and children, enabling them to grow into adulthood. These children suffer guilt, feel diminished, unworthy of his attention, ashamed of him. They may hide all this, especially if mother's behaviour implies that all must suffer in silence, or, more insidiously, that we're better off without him thank you. Meanwhile they may secretly believe themselves responsible: it was their fault for having been naughty, or unattractive, or too attractive, or for having disliked him, or disliked her. They develop a model of wife-husband behaviour (which all parents provide for their children) that makes marriage difficult for them later on. Conflict in marriage will tend to spell disaster, rather than be seen as potentially fruitful. It is hard for them to allow their internalised mother and father figures, or the feminine and masculine, to come together in their psyche and in their emotional and sexual development.[2]

There can, of course, be substitution, partial compensation: other men – like Polydectes – may be adopted as stepfathers, guides, models. Accepting and using them well will depend on how well the children, and their mother, have separated from and mourned the missing father. Too easily the family can develop an unreality, an idealism, around the absent father, the might-have-been. It is important that they learn to accept that their absent failed god-hero is but an ordinary man, and then go on to accept relationships with other ordinary men.

The sea-chest is a good image of the situation of a family in crisis: it tends to enclose itself emotionally for mutual protection, blindly preoccupied, unable to move as a coherent unit in any perceived direction. This inevitable stage of depression needs acknowledging: each one feels like a failure, a rejected victim, if the experience is not recognised as fundamentally creative. All crisis is a time of danger and opportunity. If this part of the family's journey takes them to the other shore with strength to face its further phases, then they are all growing and learning in ways which will ultimately be rewarding. The 'other shore' will be the place where life opens out, and standing on newly accepted ground, they can cultivate more direct, inventive and realistic ways of relating to one another and to the world. Children who come through such experiences are maturer than many of their more sheltered and protected peers and can contribute invaluably to a society which is undergoing the stress and instability they have as individuals learned to live with. The mother who can bear this in mind will gain strength in the role she has to play. She needs to recognise herself as in a process, and let go to that – not attempt to solve everything and wreck her own life and strength trying to compensate for what the family has lost. There is no full compensation. There are other gains.

The experience is different for a woman who is a single mother from the start. It's more likely that this is happening by choice. There tends to be more support and sympathy for the mother of a newborn baby, and she herself, being younger, may have more strength to cope and the opportunity to find friends and lovers to meet her emotional needs. However, the mystery of parenthood, the blood-connection, can't be denied. There is always the spectre of the absent father, more or less repressed, and the child, on growing older, is bound to want to know who and what he is.

Meanwhile the too-close connection with mother will need to be broken repeatedly throughout life. The fatherless only child, caught from birth onwards in a tight bond of love and pain, as Perseus doubtless was in the sea-chest, will always find it hard to make those breaks – men in particular. Some don't ever find themselves as men, and remain forever in a state of sonhood, little-boyhood, or an uncomfortable 'effeminacy'. The sympathy and devotion, the revulsion and guilt they often feel for the idealised courageous and self-denying mother who raised them makes it difficult for them to separate from her. Without a Polydectes they will not be led to face the Medusa.

'As far back as I can remember', said one such man, 'I was locked into her life. I couldn't get a detachment on it – I never saw her in relation to another adult, or to a man, so I was swallowed into her view of her reality – and boy, was that some scene . . .'

As we have already seen, such men may be carrying the frustrated need for freedom of their mothers and therefore are not free themselves, and often out of touch with their own angry frustration, their hatred of this bond. Many find their way into therapy: they have a kind of dazed, directionless quality, often a passive gentleness punctuated by unfocused violent feelings or acts, and they experience impotence of one kind or another. They lack a model, and reinforcement, of male potency.

Yet the particular nature of this maternal love and nurturing, which is inspired by the god, not by an inadequate or corrupt father, marks out these children of the feminine. They have, like Perseus, a 'special' quality, an innocence, being born of a kind of idealism. This applies too to the son of a very weak or much absent father: the well-known case of D. H. Lawrence can be seen in his novel *Sons and Lovers*. Provided the further stages of their development, as taken by Perseus, are experienced, they go on to become innovators, creators, making shift in unfamiliar circumstances, knowing how to live with instability and be unconventional without guilt: illegitimate in the best sense. Perseus, as we have seen, has the spirit of the youth of the 1960s. In the 1970s and 1980s they are maturing: dealing with the later stages of his journey.[3] Behind and within and beyond these two energies, of positive and negative 'femininity', the son of a single mother has the opportunity to find and re-define himself as a man. And Perseus has a capacity for creative destruction in the cause of evolution. To quote from Judith Arcana:

Audre Lorde has said, 'The sons of lesbians are trail-blazers, having to make their own definitions of self as men . . . sons of lesbians have the advantage of our blueprint for survival, but they must take what we know and transpose it into maleness.' Most mothers of sons are not lesbians – but all of us can heed these words. We all have to make blueprints for survival, and all our sons must take what we know – if they would make new men of themselves.[4]

So Danae, in the sea-chest, needs to trust that if she cannot make meaning out of what is happening, her son will.

The other shore: Seriphos and the shadow father

Who then is standing on the shore when Danae reaches it? She is likely to be both relieved and frightened: ready to mistrust anyone who comes to meet her – particularly any man: it will be his territory. Women who have felt betrayed by their father or their children's father find it hard ever to trust men again. However, in a firmly patriarchal society such as Danae's, a protector, and a substitute father for her child, must be found. It is still largely true today, for men still own and direct most of the world we live in. A woman who wishes for independence has to be constantly on the alert for those who do not want her to have it. So, wary of being manipulated, she may like Danae set herself on a course of defensive self-protection, openly or covertly rejecting male authority. She may, unfortunately, reject male support when she could benefit from it. At the present time, in any honest confrontation between men and women (for instance, in work-shops and conferences addressing these problems) the mistrust of men by women is only equalled by the men's bewilderment as to how to divest themselves of powers they have so long held.

The men's conflict is reflected in the two brothers on Seriphos, the two father-figures who receive Danae. There is the sympathetic 'good father'-ly Dictys, who rescues and welcomes her, but is too poor to keep her, and the patronising seductive 'bad father' King Polydectes, generous but proud and controlling. Many men are caught between these two kinds of patronage. Danae must accept the King's patronage. But she will not marry him: she maintains her independence. She is bound to feel resistance to a man who so resembles her father and wields a similar authority. And after having been divinely loved she cannot accept a mortal mate, nor a human to father the son of a god. So she preserves her sense of rightness, her devotion.

This preservation of purity by Danae is a significant element in Perseus's growth. Her devotion and perseverance suggest how discrimination coupled with obstinacy will prevail in the face of seduction when a child, or a creative project, is being nurtured. She

31

will not sell herself, but maintains her own personal freedom and conviction and values – her sense of self – and by implication her child's.

There are many such Danaes today, who choose to remain unmarried and perhaps celibate also, out of a similar determination not to undersell themselves but to hold on to their integrity. For many it is a painful choice: and it involves a loss of vitality, but it is a way of declaring and holding to the spiritual quality of their sexuality, to Danae's knowledge of Zeus, a woman's conviction that sex without love, a regard for the whole person, is degrading, and to be treated as a possession by a man is unholy. The sad paradox is that only by giving up sex or marriage can they insist on the quality, the equality of sexual relating.

In the situation of having to relate to Polydectes, Danae is bound to feel the distress and tension of their conflict. Perseus and Polydectes feel it too. Danae may be tempted to yield, and then become egotistical in her 'superiority'. She may be aware that Polydectes loves and desires her genuinely but is slave to his own conditioning, seeing sex as a matter of power and conquest. Compromise seems impossible to either. This kind of tension between the sexes is a fundamental one, and like all conflict it is potentially creative. Woman, for whom body, spirit and nurturing are deeply interconnected, will always experience conflict with man, for whom mind, detachment and purpose tend to be split off from bodily experience. Yet she needs him to contain and bring order to her sometimes blindly passionate wholeness – even divert her from it – just as he needs her to mediate for him with the world of expansive and inclusive emotion in which he often feels at sea.[5] Ideally their energies should be complementary, reflecting as they do right- and left-brain activity in each individual. Perseus and Andromeda will achieve that later.

Of course these conflicts between men and women have been the stuff of myth and literature for centuries. But they are reaching a crucial point now, and Perseus will have to extricate himself from this complex. D. M. Thomas, in a very illuminating article on the present situation, writes thus:

> Since we have never more desperately needed the unashamed woman to help bring the world back to sanity. I hate to see her trying to escape from her sexuality – even though I understand

the reasons. The real equality of the sexes, which I want to see translated into every area of life, is not threatened by a woman's sexual fantasy of submission . . . If an ardent feminist wants to imagine that her lover is taking her against her will, it should be seen as a game, a ritual drama . . .

It's a game that Adam and Lilith played. I'm sure they both enjoyed it. But someone, later – a man – got screwed-up, and altered the record. Woman, made to feel guilty, drew back her sexuality, and the man who had caused it, emotionally deprived, played with his toys, built his models – even to today's final, most deadly phallic symbol.[6]

No doubt that Polydectes is only too willing to send Perseus off to nuclear war. But we must acknowledge Danae's complicity, and if we return to the story and look at it at an interpersonal level the pattern becomes clearer.

Polydectes's structure contains Danae and her son until the crisis when Perseus comes to maturity. He becomes caught in the conflict and a very familiar triangular situation arises as he grows through adolescence. It happens today not just in the particular setting of an unmarried or divorced mother and her son, but also where a mother has a favoured son who understands her frustrated aspirations better than her husband. A woman with a despised or unacceptable mate binds her son to herself and he becomes her protector and substitute husband. Father or stepfather grows increasingly jealous and seeks to undermine or oust the son: and indeed the son must ultimately take up the older man's challenge – as Perseus does – to leave his mother and prove himself a man.

The pain of this situation will be acute wherever wife and husband are not sufficiently 'together' because of his weakened potency or authority at home. There is no male succession in this structure: unless there is a work-area which is a shared male domain – i.e. a 'kingdom' – be it a family business or an accepted and mutually valued way of life for the men, then the negotiation for succession between father and son, needed as the son grows to manhood, can't happen: it focuses instead on the regressive situation of the emotional relationship with mother.[7] So the father who could share his own potency with his growing son, helping to empower him, instead uses his power to banish him, send him defenceless out into the world, or abandon him, defenceless to stand up to his overpowering mother. In the myth, the mother takes two forms: Danae chaste, tender, unselfish, and Medusa sexual, destructive, terrifying. Polydectes seeks to sacrifice Perseus (who will not be heir to the throne – certainly if Danae doesn't marry him) to the dark feminine power that has become a monstrous threat to masculinity. Part of woman's sexual power is, of course, that of producing male heirs. If her fertility is dried up she can indeed undermine patriarchy.

There are interesting parallels here with the story of *Hamlet*. In Shakespeare's play we can see Danae and Medusa in Gertrude, Andromeda in Ophelia. Hamlet's succession to the throne is in dispute. The stepfather Claudius sends Hamlet away hoping for his death, but the plan backfires, as it does for Polydectes. Hamlet however never resolves the problem of the Medusa of perverted sexuality: his mother has sold herself. So Hamlet is unable to 'rescue' Ophelia and his own inner feminine. He is caught, as is Shakespeare, in the patriarchal trap.

Recognising this triangular conflict in all its complexities is vital to progress; it needs to be transcended: Perseus must leave it. Sometimes the parents are so blindly stuck in the situation that he isn't kicked out. Or he leaves taking the conflict with him, internalised, unsolved, for ever blocking his self-realisation. Again the drama of the bickering parents takes attention from the child's real needs.

A single mother may find Danae and Polydectes in conflict within herself. Once she recognises and owns this she will be able to exercise the male function and send her son away, lest he cling too long to her. This may not happen until she realises how the Danae within her is subtly hanging on to this 'ideal' son, who is much easier to relate to than any ordinary mortal man of her own generation. (She has, after all, made him in her own image.) Without the safety of their mutual attachment, mother and son will both be up against the harsh realities, the rough-and-tumble of men/women relationships, the pains and problems of sexual freedom. Danae will want to hang on, for her life experience and her age will not give cause for optimism. Her anxiety about her own future is a depressing context for her son, who misses a father's cheerful encouragement and guidance to support him in his ventures into adult life. But, however ill-equipped, he needs to go: his age is right for taking on the challenge.

Perseus independent

From now on Perseus is at the centre of the story. Only when the fatherless youth has left home can he develop his own personality and forge the direction and meaning of his life. Home has involved an ideal image of the good self-sacrificing mother which they have both been preserving, and the first things he will have to deal with are the negative and sexual aspects of woman which have been concealed. Such men do tend to find, or arouse, the Medusa in the women they relate to. One extreme version of this is, 'Mother was so perfect no other woman can come up to her – and sexual women are seductive traitors.' So they are drawn to mother-figures, or to cold, sexually tantalising women. They behave childishly and arouse the woman's hostility. They withdraw and punish her, and she gets back at them . . . When their relationships with women prove untenable these men may turn to psychotherapy for help. They are led to confront the dark mother, and like the Medusa she turns out to be far more than just their own one personal mother or wife. In the next two chapters we shall examine more closely the nature of Medusa and the creative outcome of Perseus's meeting with her.

At the same time this quasi-hero has to develop his own concept of the masculine also, and to come to terms with the absent fathers. Uninfluenced by mother's prejudices, he will be able to construct his own version of manhood and fatherhood – which is what so many men are now having to do. Betrayal is very often a necessary part of the process (Hillman 1964). The patriarchs betray the young men, sending them to the slaughter, to the Gorgons' cave, to the Somme, to Vietnam. When father–son trust is ruptured, new meanings must be made, new forms and structures for living. Exploring the nature of father becomes in itself an act of fathering.

Perseus proceeds, as we shall see, partly by following his destiny, partly by trial and error, finding assistance where he can, using ingenuity, Dutch courage and inspired intelligence. This is a process of self-formation, self-definition. It is akin to the self-creation of the goddess described in chapter 2, and it is Athena, a wisdom-goddess, who guides him. Perls describes it thus: 'The self is precisely the integrator . . . the artist of life . . . it plays a crucial role of finding and making the meanings we grow by' (Perls, Hefferline and

Goodman 1973). Coleridge, one hundred and fifty years before him, said, '. . . It is even this that constitutes genius – the power of acting creatively under laws of its own origination.'[8]

In that sense Perseus has genius – but so have we all when the emergency of father's absence and betrayal is upon us. Though I shall look more closely in chapter 11 at what the myth tells us about creative process, it must be already apparent that Perseus is indeed now a creative artist, innovator, and also a symbol of a creative project (his parents'): his work is original, originating, it is not bound by outworn ideas. Somehow he is going to find a place of authority (authoring, fathering) which honours what he is, within or without a patriarchy that has disowned him. His experience of a matriarch will influence him, and the way will be manifest in his destined role as destroyer.

We begin to see how Perseus can serve as a model of the kind of spiritual heroism we need in our own time. The similarities with Jesus are there: the differences are important. Patriarchal monotheism has ultimately led to the critical situation our world is in. Jehovah is more like Acrisius than any of the gods – and the gods always had the goddesses around to keep some balance. Jesus's martyrdom is very like the martyrdom of woman, of the feminine in Christianity. But Perseus signally avoids becoming a scapegoat or martyr. He stands for life and self-renewal, not the cult of sacrifice. His mother and wife are saved by him from degradation and death, his daughter refuses to be sacrificed. Our civilisation sorely needs to stop cultivating and identifying with the persecuted Christ-figure. The greater task, of staying alive, while co-existing with the Medusa, requires all the creativity we can muster.

Chapter 5

Medusa and Athena:
The perversion of love and fertility

When we come to the Medusa, we see how all the critical problems that have been accumulating for Perseus have come to a head. If we try to examine who or what she is, we find that the quantity and diversity of interpretations, ideas and projections that have attached themselves to her notorious figure are daunting.

That statement contains all the truth about the Medusa: the need to look at her because she is there, the terrifying head she has developed, and the way she overwhelmingly threatens to paralyse us.

Her story is of particular significance. Athena and Poseidon had competed for the patronage of the city which subsequently became Athens. When he lost the contest, Poseidon, who had a reputation for belligerence and misogyny, showed his defiance by making love to Medusa on the altar of Athena's temple. She was a mortal, connected with the cult of earth- and moon-goddesses. Athena, outraged, took her revenge on her: she turned her beautiful hair into writhing snakes, and put her in a cave to become the third of the Gorgon sisters (the other two were immortal). Anyone who looked at her was turned to stone.

Her condition, then, is the product of jealousy, insult and envy: the male god's envy of the goddess, and Athena's envious attack on Medusa's sexuality, on her earth and moon qualities. Athena, goddess of war and wisdom, sprang fully armed from her father Zeus's forehead – a mental product, a daughter of the patriarch, who refused to allow any god or man to love her sexually. In this instance she punishes not the male perpetrator of the defilement of her temple, but the woman.

This is a fair picture of the way a woman can pervert and corrupt her own beauty and sexuality out of anger at men. From her intellect and mental pride she may reject and spoil her own body. She may indeed cut her hair back severely, unable to allow either the beauty or the ugliness of Medusa's locks to be a visible part of her personality. It happens when she feels threatened by forces over which she has no control: the oceanic, orgasmic power, the brute strength of Poseidon, which she fears to call up in a man and also has within herself. There are Athena elements in the feminist movement, denying the spiritual and sexual power of woman, interested only in emulating, defying and competing with men. They turn themselves into Medusas and present a real threat to any man or man-loving woman who dares to come near.

The snakes, though they have their phallic associations, are a reminder of awesome snake-goddess qualities, and in some traditions the Medusa is honoured for that. So it could be said that the Medusa is cursed and cursing, in the way that menstruation is branded 'the curse': feminine power is invalidated and given a bad name. Medusa, the Gorgon, came to represent all that was terrifying about the female genitalia, menstruation and the dark mother: fascinating, mysterious, potentially death-dealing, castrating, disempowering.[1]

The Medusa, then, is a woman with a reputation. She has been scapegoated, and like any scapegoat nothing but ill is said of her: she takes all kinds of negative projections. The first were from Athena, and from Poseidon, who made love to her partly out of hatred, abandoned her, and laid her open to abuse. So she has taken their poison into herself, and it turns into a bitter envy which attacks and paralyses those who look at her. As Melanie Klein put it – and her work on envy is very revealing for an understanding of the Medusa – envious attacks 'are directed not only against the individual's aggression but also, and even predominantly, against the individual's progressive and creative capacities'.[2] The Medusa has been attacked that way and now attacks herself and others similarly.

Her experience was painfully familiar to one woman who had suffered sexual abuse by her vindictive Poseidon-like stepfather during her adolescence:

'My mother was well-meaning, but, yes, a real Athena: holier-than-thou, puritanical. He'd behave like an animal – all his base instincts came out. She was frustrating him sexually, so he took it out on me. Then of course she turned on me too – really vicious – I hadn't expected that. Threw me out. Between them they really messed me up. I can't get it right. The men are all over me – but it always goes wrong. So I go completely frigid and seize up and won't go near them. Yet I'd love to marry and have children.'

It is said of Medusa that she is longing to love, and longing to give birth to the child she has got from Poseidon. So she is the exact negative of Danae: pregnant with the god's child, but unable to bring forth, consequently full of distress, hatred and envy of all those 'normal' people she sees.

The Medusa represents blocked and self-blocking creativity, stifled and warped fecundity, spiritual constipation. She is the mother who threatens that we will be killed in wanting to be born, such as the one described in chapter 2. She has suffered such punishment from the envious or vengeful masculine elements in her world, or in her own psyche or personality, that life is petrified and killed off in her presence. And it is her head that is in its ugliness compelled to project out on to others the meaningless pain of her body: the relationship between her head and the rest of her body is profoundly sick: her mind cannot cope, and indeed she needs the outsider Perseus to make meaning of her suffering.

It is no wonder that the Medusa has been a source of fascination for centuries: she is so recognisable, in ourselves as in others. Participants in workshops readily identified with her complex, distressing qualities of sourness and illwill arising from frustration of the need to love, the paralysing power she exerts, the destructive depressing killjoy effect. They felt how easily it could annihilate the vitality and creativity of others, as well as their own. She felt unmoving, immovable, holding on to herself, stuck, full of festering poison. One person described it in a poem:

> I am stone
> stone stone
> hard granite
> trapped
> unmoving

I am taut
stone stone
clenched unyielding
jailed
rigid

I am negative energy
moving upwards
stone in my eyes
I freeze you
You cannot approach me

I turn you to granite
I make you unyielding
locked together in a living deadness
no escape
but knowledge
somehow
of softer feelings

a fluid moving interior
that is the last
vestige of life[3]

The physical pathology of the Medusa condition takes many forms. The emotional state is almost always accompanied by some kind of sickness which increasingly debilitates the body (see chapter 12). Energy-flow is blocked, life-aggression turned inward, motility is rigidified by the accompanying fear. The body attacks itself, as it does in extreme afflictions like arthritis, ulcers, cancer. Indeed the Medusa's significance is in displaying how the perversion of the body's potential spirituality produces sickness. Dealing with the Medusa, dealing with wasting diseases, involves a painful revaluation of our attitudes to our bodies.

Marion Woodman explores this as it relates to women in particular in her two books which are especially concerned with anorexia and obesity (Woodman 1980, 1982). The second looks at the Athena, Medusa and Andromeda archetypes in relation to woman's self-image and the repression of the feminine. In writing of 'the anguish of the writhing Medusa' she relates it to the increasing addictiveness of our society.

... the once beautiful Medusa, whose snaky locks twist and
writhe in constant agitation, reaching, reaching, reaching,
wanting more and more and more ... she is so angry and so full
of repressed energy that to face her brings on a paralysis of fear.[4]

In all the Medusa's pathological forms the tension of holding,
and the increasing anxious obsession with the body itself, are
maintained by very restricted breathing – a literal blocking of
inspiration and aspiration, of the spiritual, and vitality. The body
has wellnigh ceased to be a vessel of the spirit.

This blocking of the spirit, the control and suppression of
breathing and space to breathe, is a feature of a soulless society
which thwarts and abuses free creativity. Woman's creativity
especially is repressed by dominant men. Many fathers, absent or
present, act from womb envy. In today's world women are
frequently invited into projects by men, only to have their more
attractive ideas appropriated and their true feminine strengths
ignored. Like Medusa they are robbed of their potential child, and
easily become eaten up with concealed anger and jealousy as they
watch the man enjoying the prestige and the satisfaction of his
work, blind to how much richer it could be were he to collaborate
genuinely and imaginatively with the woman. Complaints are
interpreted as pettiness or hysteria or trendy feminism and the
woman, conditioned to submit and take a back seat, is alienated,
driven into the Gorgons' cave, where she plagues herself and others
with her negativity and spitefulness.[5]

The subjugated goddess or priestess can turn into a dangerous
witch. The history is there, and woman carries it in her unconscious:
in the Middle Ages the fear of woman's sexual and spiritual power
led to the devaluation and debasement of feminine mysteries, of
witchcraft with its potential for healing, to the scapegoating,
persecution, torture and murder of a million ordinary women
under Christian patriarchal rule.[6] Women were warned off and
have hardly recovered from the imprinted fear.

Mass witchhunting has ceased, but in more recent, individualistic
times, the Medusa process can be seen in the lives of women artists
or writers, some of them sisters, wives or mistresses of famous
creative men. There are many whose talents have gone uncelebrated
in a patriarchal literary and artistic culture which increasingly
places value on fame, achievement, bestselling, products. The

creative expression of these women becomes vitiated, leading them sometimes to insanity. It is invariably the projection on to the woman of the man's feared impotence, feared non-productivity, and there has been no Perseus for them. Esther Kreitman, sister of the two Bashevis Singers, was one such, a gifted writer who ended her days in mental derangement.[7] Vivien Eliot clearly took over the dark goddess aspects of her husband T. S. Eliot and acted out the Medusa he could not handle in himself, finally going into insanity.[8] One of the most interesting examples in this context of the myth is that of Camille Claudel, an outstanding sculptor. (It's worth noting that for these three women the Medusa complex was constellated around the time of the First World War.)

Camille Claudel was the older sister of the celebrated writer and diplomat Paul Claudel and for ten years mistress and close associate of Auguste Rodin. Her relationship with her brother was a powerful one with clearly incestuous undertones. Their mother, Athena-like, had no time for her daughter's audacious creativity. Their father encouraged his children's talents – but he absented himself, separating from the family when Camille was 18. Shortly after this she left home, to the distress of Paul, and went to live with Rodin.

The artistic liaison with Rodin was clearly symbiotic: it is hard to tell, looking at her extraordinary, vital, frankly sexual sculpture, who inspired whom, or who was the more powerful and accomplished artist. He was of course the famous one. Like the Medusa she did not enjoy the full fruits of her creativity. Indeed she is believed to have borne Rodin a child which was adopted out, and possibly to have had another aborted. The disapproval of her conventional environment and of her mother perverted her fertility. Rodin used her. (It is interesting that on the two occasions she served as model for him he sculpted her head only and set it in a block of stone . . .)

After separating from Rodin, Camille lived alone, and in course of time became increasingly disturbed, intensely paranoid in relation to him, his reputation and her work, and finally a sick self-destructive recluse. She was committed to an asylum, a few days after her father died, at the age of 49: no doubt her psychotic condition was influenced by the menopause also (see next chapter). When, after two years, she seemed recovered, the doctors recommended she go home to her family. Her mother would not take her and refused to give permission for her to leave. She remained in the asylum another thirty years until she died, never sculpting again, her life petrified.

The last major sculpture Camille Claudel produced before her insanity was a striking lifesize statue of Perseus slaying the Medusa. He seems almost to rise himself out of her decapitated body, and he holds her head above and behind him while staring at it in the mirror-shield. The head, with its mad staring squinted eyes, is Camille's own, a grim prophetic self-portrait. The eyes have the quality we associate with paranoid schizophrenia, reflecting and shrinking from the eyes of the mother who, professing love, stares at her infant with hatred (a fundamental schizophrenogenic situation), which would tally with Camille's experience of her own mother, and of having as a mother discarded or aborted her own babies: the Medusa condition.

Camille in her own subsequent life could only be the stuck Medusa, not released or redeemed by any Perseus. Rodin and Claudel pursued their creativity elsewhere: both felt guilty about her fate but were obviously threatened by her condition, haunted by their complicity in it, and too trapped by their cultural conditioning to want to help liberate her genius and grant her happiness. Thus the Medusa state is compounded.[9]

This is an especially dramatic example, highlighted by artistic awareness, of how Medusas are made. But in many ordinary homes, in less publicised contexts, Medusas develop in mothers whose husbands have abandoned the family. The divorced woman will often become aggrieved and bitter at the curb put on her children's development by the man who seems to have – indeed has – robbed her of her potential creativity. Twenty or more years of her life will be taken up with a project – the family – that will never meet the hopes she had for it. Taken over by her own inner revengeful rational Athena (for whom all must go according to her set plan) she gets stuck in her grudge, becomes the heavy self-righteous mother, and is unable to free herself or her family for new living or for other creative activity. Paranoid feelings about the missing father fill the loneliness she experiences: he may in reality be attacking her subtly from the sidelines. This too is an abuse of matriarchy and fertility. The maternal is given undue power, and the free spirituality of woman's nature is denied. The body, food, material concerns predominate: liberation of the spirit or of the sexuality of mother and children is not on the agenda. The incestuous binding is similar to Acrisius's regime. The overpowering American Mom, the smothering Jewish mother, the uptight controlling British motherdear, have these Medusa qualities. And the distressed middle-aged or menopausal woman has become a classic manifestation of the sickness of our misogynist society. This I shall consider in the next chapter.

This insidious process, taken for granted, unnamed, its dangers unrecognised, expands, escalates, until we are suddenly faced with a Medusa on a global scale. At the moment she manifests in terrorist militarism, in economic depression, in Third World dereliction, the spectre of nuclear or ecological annihilation, all of which stem from materialism and the misuse of the earth's resources, and of human – feminine – creativity.

In the 1930s and 1940s the Nazi regime, the most monstrous manifestation of evil in our time, was undoubtedly the result of the brutal repression of the feminine by soul-destroying patriarchies: the subjugation of German women, the excessive cultivation of rationalism, the impoverishment and stifled creativity of a richly cultured nation after World War I due to the Allies' envy, negative projection, scapegoating, disowning their own misdemeanours. So the Medusa of Nazism, driven relentlessly by corrosive envy, destroyed millions of healthy souls and paralysed humanity's trust in itself. Part of the Nazi cult was of an Athena-like womanhood, alongside indulgence in black magic, and a perversion of human power and sexuality in the ghastly studied and meaningless sadism of the concentration camps. And we are still haunted by it, for the Medusa will not let us go until we confront her and recognise how we made her what she is. We are indeed in danger of being paralysed by the enormity of the holocaust and by the horror of nuclear destruction that was invented to counteract it. The psychologist Nicholas Humphrey has spoken of it thus:

> We behave at times as though we have been hexed by the Bomb, put under a spell . . . The Bomb is patently a superhuman weapon: mind-blowingly destructive – and, if we so see it, mind-blowingly magnificent. Small wonder if people's fear is mixed with awe, if they become hypnotised by the Bomb's dread beauty and its fascinating power.[10]

His words might well be describing the Medusa and those who look on her.

'Hateful outside – loving inside' was the way one person described what it felt like to be the Medusa. The problem is to recognise and release that loving impulse and cultivate it, within ourselves and others. The fascination of the serpents, of remembered and potential evil, becomes obsessive: monstrosity is held in awe, cynicism kills off all optimism and trust in the simplicity of movement outwards and towards others, of the healing power of the heart, of love and human warmth, and we are in the Gorgons' cave with the mentality of Polydectes. Yet the Perseus in us, divinely fathered, knows something else, knows that there is a god's child even in a Medusa.

Maurice Friedman writes of the 'hidden human image' – of our lost benign image of ourselves.[11] Perseus is looking for it, for he has to find a human form for his manhood. The image itself, in an age of pervasive, invasive television, has the hold on us that myth had for the Greeks. The television set in our homes has become like a Medusa, staring back at us with its negative portrayals of human life, its concentration on violence and disaster, its corruption of sex and love and of the creativity of those who work for it, its materialist and commercialist values. If we stare too hard and come to believe that this is reality, not myth, the Medusa has us in her grip. If we use the television image as Athena's mirror-shield, to reflect on our realities, myths and images, then we can survive, as Perseus does. Even Athena, in her wisdom, and perhaps with remorse, knew there was a way round, other truths than the inevitable destructivity of the Medusa, so she offered him a way of finding another truth. Athena's relation to the Medusa is the mind's relation to the body and its control over that relationship. Perseus, by dislodging the Athena-Medusa complex, releases the spirit.

Chapter 6

Generation and regeneration
Perseus the creative destroyer

What does Perseus consciously know? The myth doesn't tell us; his lack of knowledge must increase his fear. Does he know what the oracle told Acrisius? Or the history of the Medusa? He is someone whose progress in life is based on a combination of conscious and unconscious awareness. At this point he is the young male, still uncertain how to assert himself, unsure of what is happening to him. For such uncertain states of awareness there is no language; the concepts have hardly formed. This in itself puts him at risk with a rock-hard wily Medusa (her name means 'cunning'), who signally is a fixed concept. In one workshop a Medusa dismissed him scornfully: 'He really is a *wimp*.' Someone pointed out that the wimp was about to kill her.

Perseus has come from a situation of betrayal by Polydectes who has taken advantage of his innocence and rashness, yet he is determined to fulfil the supposedly impossible mission; he exerts his ingenuity and draws on unfamiliar energies. He has to have faith in himself, and in the goddess Athena. He trusts the feminine, the goddess who is, like himself, a child of Zeus. This faith is in direct contrast to Polydectes' willingly pessimistic belief in the indestructibility of the Medusa. ('My ex-husband's afraid of me,' said one woman. 'He tried to warn my son off this terrible woman. But in fact my son and I get on OK. We understand one another. If I get too much for him he just shuts me up.') Perseus knows there is love behind the Medusa's destructiveness, and is aware at some level of consciousness of the divine child trapped unborn within her. Here in the dark womb-like cave he will recall how he too was once trapped, unborn, in Danae's womb. He will recognise the rigid mother, constricted by the traitor father, who might well have overwhelmed and killed him had not the god-given life force carried him forward to survival. He will see the hitherto unrecognised negative holding power of the Danae he has just left, the unacknowledged incestuous sexuality between his mother and himself, which is manifest in the threatening and fascinating serpents, the only moving energy in that deathly body. Reflection in the mirror reveals his own blocked sexuality and creativity.

'Hitherto unrecognised' is the essence of what the myth of Medusa tells us: that energies and negativities that we suppress, conceal or ignore, idealising our own innocence, are projected outwards on to someone, or some power, that becomes corrupted. It is a matter of life and death that Perseus confront the Medusa, lest he fall victim to that destructive power.

These are some of the impressions of the meeting of Perseus and the Medusa, from a number of men and women identifying with both:

Medusa:
'Everyone and everything is closing in on me. Black-arrows – strong feeling of the blue core in me. Maybe it's my emptiness. A hollow person.

My breathing is imprisoned.

Powerful feeling of focusing anger through my eyes on Perseus. Beautiful core in me. Can't ever take away that goodness and beauty no matter what you see. Awed by my ability to be so powerful. No desire to harm Perseus.

Saviour boy, not enemy, kill me, that I may love again.

Hate myself – repulsive – kill – intensity – hope/fear – expectation of rejection. I hate you because you can't love me/ release me. So I don't want you to exist, remind me of what I can't have/achieve.'

Perseus:
'I have come to destroy her. That is my mission. I will not let her destroy me. What was it those others saw in her, that gave her such power to fright them out of life? What did they not see? People can be so blind.

Don't suffocate me: I'm not going to be devoured by you.

49

This is her outside only, her reflection. I feel hatred, anger, danger, turmoil. I can't see inside her.
We are united in terror.
I see yearning eyes, longing for release.
My mirror, my stare, reflects softness, and remorse.
In that stance, I see dancing
And in that stony glare, I see air.
I am Perseus. And I am excited. Can I do what no man has done? Can I survive? Can I kill?'

Perseus has been given: by Hermes, a sickle to sever the Medusa's head; by the Stygian nymphs, a pouch to put the head in, a cloak of invisibility, and wings for his feet, to escape pursuit by the other Gorgons; and by Athena, the mirror-shield.

The mirror-shield: protection and reflection. He can look at the Medusa at a remove, without fear of death, hold her image in his grasp, assess what she is, gain understanding and resolve: the accuracy and strength required to slay her. He sees himself also in the mirror, realises this frightening creature beside him is no more nor less than he himself: they have the same capacity to destroy, the same envy and hatred of the betraying fathers, the same impotence and blocked fertility. And in the mirror he can see the differences: his youthful, less corrupted nature, his maleness, the features of the god his father, his innate goodwill, optimism, looking forward to life, not death. The hidden human image, once revealed, comprises positive and negative, innocence and experience, youth and age, female and male.

The mirror-shield is about images, imagining and imagination: it is about illusion also, and disillusion, and the nature of our perceptions of reality. It serves Perseus as a medium, bridging the gap between inner and outer reality, between the inner known and the outer unknown, between life and death. To live fully, we must be able to contemplate death.

There are many such media, symbolic phenomena which allow us to reflect on our realities and fantasies: they are central to our creative life: 'areas of permitted illusion', as Winnicott terms them in *Playing and Reality*, a book which deals extensively with this border country of experiencing (Winnicott 1971: I discuss this in more detail in chapter 11). Dreams are the most powerful; fantasy, language, psychotherapy, poetry and other arts, myth itself, play, humour, scientific exploration, politics, military encounters, forms of culture, including agriculture and horticulture: these are all means by which we try to come to terms with the chaos of human existence and find a form to give it order, keep it in manageable proportions: the Medusa contained in a mirror-shield.

Crucial to the use of the shield is that we recognise its indirectness, that Perseus knows it is a medium, not giving him the reality (his death under her gaze). And all reality is relative. Paradoxically the Medusa herself, a projection of his and others' fantasies, is only dangerous if she is submitted to by those who choose to enter her notorious cave believing in her reputation. This is the danger of 'symbolic equation', which I've mentioned in connection with television. The myth is taken for real.[1]

The mirror-shield is a 'transitional object', as defined by Winnicott,[2] which enables us to move on in our process of ego-formation, of maturing and separating out our own personality. By looking in it Perseus will realise how much the negative of Danae has been introjected within him, and is a projection of his own negativities, and this is the crucial point of separation from her, lest he be stuck, paralysed by this holding symbiosis. Cutting off her head will be like cutting the cord. (In psychotherapy the therapist acts as the mirror-shield, taking the Medusa projections and helping to transform them in the transference.) One young man said:

> 'It was only when I looked coolly at my mother's self-destructive grudge against my father that I realised what I saw was what I'd been doing myself . . . I dropped out of training as an architect after he left us. He'd always encouraged me in it. But he abandoned me: he'd shown me what it was to be effective in the world, then left me to it – incomplete. I was so bitter I refused to complete it, refused to complete anything. I hated the idea of being successful. And I suspect she almost *wanted* me to be a failure, just to show him . . .'

What of the cloak of invisibility? It suggests what may happen when we seek to avoid the destructive Medusa – we may need to hide, become invisible, for a while losing all sense of who we are, avoid the dangers of the confrontation even though we are impelled to confront. Men in particular tend to 'disappear' in such situations, to tell lies, escape the emotional pressure – their only defence perhaps in some circumstances. A woman colleague once observed to me that young men never looked her in the face when talking about their mothers or about her: not only do they keep their heads turned away, like Perseus, but she is prevented from seeing in their faces what is going on in them: they have become invisible. (Perhaps in general at present the younger male adopts a safe cloak of invisibility while the Medusas of feminism have their eye on him.)

It was a woman, however, who though she knew nothing of the Medusa myth, came to a condition of invisibility in a fantasy pursued in a therapy session – and this is a good example of the use of a symbolic medium, a mirror-shield, for she had no other way of facing the sense of doom and death she was experiencing in spite of the brightness of the hopeful rich life she was leading. She felt that underneath the beautiful 'superstructures' of her world (she and her family were about to move into a lovely new home) there were dark underground depths. Invited to enter them, she visualised herself going deep into dark, cold caves and finding at the end an old, wasted crone, repulsive, marble-eyed, whose deathly gaze terrified her, and promised that however frequently she might manage to escape the deathly power would keep drawing her back, and ultimately get her in its grasp. In her fear she turned herself invisible and allowed herself to flow back, as blood, to the entrance of the cave. There she became a rock, safe in the moonlight. She knew she would have to return according to the moon-cycles. The connection with menstruation is evident. And perhaps the cloak of invisibility is some form of psychic, or real, contraception. The sperm, the life-force represented by Perseus, knows it goes to its potential death when it creates life, and can only gamble on what life it might be creating, so it attempts to vanish even as it advances. He inherits his father Zeus's elusiveness.

It is significant that this woman's fantasy envisages a cyclical death-in-life process, so that each contact with the dark witch is a rehearsal for the final end of life, which meanwhile goes on, unaware, in the conscious world above; whereas the Perseus myth gives us a male who must slay death so that he may survive and be born anew. This tallies with observations that men are more concerned with death, survival and immortality (and will try to cheat death, like Acrisius) and women with birth and life-renewal within the confines of mortality.[3] We do, of course, combine both:

we go through the Perseus trip many times in the life-cycle, whenever there is a fundamental passage to be made.

There are universal implications. This woman had previously expressed many fears about nuclear warfare and the constant underlying threat to her children's future. The Bomb is a projection of humanity's explosive feelings; it is still, and hopefully will remain, a symbol, a menacing Medusa. We might think that there has to be a kind of menstrual purging of the world's sickness which will involve bloodshed, and the temporary disappearance, silent invisibility of the good elements of humanity – implicit in increased contraception, and relational sterility. Or we might, like Perseus, determine to cut off the lethal head, banish the Bomb, dissolve hawkish government, and release the global resources, the frozen assets, which have been stuck, invested in this Medusa.

The sickle comes from Hermes, who is associated, through his caduceus, with healing. It is used as in an act of surgery on a malignant growth. At times the transformation of Medusa is a slow process of putrefaction as we wait for the toxicity to work itself through: a purging. But when the accumulated poisons are more than the organism can bear, and the closed-circuit system dangerously overcharged, drastic measures are needed. The anti-life force must be destroyed. Just as in his birth Perseus, leaving a potentially toxic womb, had to violate and break through the cervix, so he must now cut through her flesh and sever the lethal head. Simulating this act in movement, we are acutely, bodily aware of the dilemma which lies behind emotional situations where we need to cut ourselves off from clinging close relatives or friends, put an end to festering relationships:

> 'I wanted to be brave, but I'm afraid. I know I have help, I know I'm strong, but I'm still afraid. What will happen? I see her. My fear is her fear. We reflect each other's fear. I know my strength and I strike out. In sheer terror.'

This is the terror that promotes acts of bravery, the fear that mobilises, doesn't paralyse or depress itself. Others shrink from the act, hesitate:

> 'I can't do it.' 'I don't like this. I haven't the skill.' 'I have to do it like an athlete performing.' 'I cut both ways.' 'Her eyes look grateful.' 'I must see properly to cut right.' 'It needs force – an act of will.'

Yet they feel the inevitability of her dying:

> 'I'm motivated by the truth.' 'I can only do it because I have faith in the outcome: that something good will come of this.'

Perseus's right arm is strong and clear once he sees the threat fully. He makes his decision, is decisive, incisive. He is a destroyer. We respect our reluctance to destroy, to kill, and we have to own the creative potential of our capacity to do so, in order to be responsibly in charge of that capacity. Abortion, suicide, euthanasia, are practices which involve assuming that responsibility. The initial tendency in the 1930s to appease the Nazi regime stemmed in part from a genuine pacifism, but that horrifying Medusa could only be disposed of by the sword, by decisive destruction.

The Medusa head is subsequently used by Perseus for other acts of destruction, and then given to Athena to be placed on her shield. For us it may represent the continuing reminder, the memory of the Medusa of the Somme, of Auschwitz and Hiroshima, which we can use with discrimination to avoid worse disasters and to destroy those shadows of evil in ourselves and our world that lead to barbarism.

Ageing women and young men: the maturing feminine and the renascent masculine

Let us look at the individual experience of Danae/Medusa and Perseus: the situation of the older woman who is unsupported by the males of her generation, the absent fathers, and of the younger man who lacks fathering yet needs some way of relating to this mother-figure without being overpowered by her. This relationship may exist between a mother and son, but also, on a wider social scale, between women who have intimate experience of the ills of patriarchy, and men who have the opportunity to develop in a different way, and avoid making the patriarchs' mistakes.

To start with, at the personal level, it is socially far more acceptable, and more common, for a young woman to be in relationship with an older man, than a young man with an older woman. Older women are cursed, like the Medusa, with a bad press. Yet in some tribes it is the honoured role of the older women to teach the erotic arts to the young man. Such an attitude is rare in Western society, where older women are largely rejected. Middle-aged and menopausal women form a high proportion of the mentally or physically sick population. GPs and psychotherapists have many such patients, predominantly suffering depression, with a variety of associated hysterical symptoms, many of them phobic or paranoid, or experiencing all the perplexing disorientations and distresses of the 'change of life'. In most cases those treating them can do little for them, and cover up their own helplessness and hostility towards these incurable Gorgons (who seem to render them impotent) by issuing tranquillisers in quantity, or consigning them to chronic invalidism.

Such women have projected on to them society's negativity – its fear of ageing and dying, its stress on productivity, its warped attitudes to the body, sex and menstruation. It devalues woman's experience, denying the importance of the spiritual; it is not interested in wisdom and mystery. The basis of woman's wisdom is her inner intuitive, heart knowledge, and inner blood knowledge; yet many women have, under patriarchy, lost contact with and confidence in that wisdom, and are forced to accept the male definitions of what they are, while they feel instinctively but inarticulately that the definition – or 'diagnosis' – is wrong.[4] They come to psychotherapy initially with symptoms, but ultimately in search of the meaning of what is happening to them – which leads to transpersonal considerations: concern with the soul. They go through the Medusa-Perseus process in order to allow the release of Pegasus, the transpersonal image of liberated spirituality and expansive energy.

The Medusa-like depressed older woman has a daunting dis-piritedness that threatens to sap the energy of all those she meets, and it's a sad reflection on our society that there is this terrible wasted resource of older women. The menopause marks a vital transition into maturity after the active family-centred, ego-centred mid-life years, and it calls for a revaluation of all those years as one begins to look towards the ending of life. For a woman (and for any man who will let it happen to him) it calls into question to what use her body and her creativity have been put, and what has happened to her soul in our soulless society, and what her identity is, if she depends on that society to define it. Where it has not been quite spent over the years, the energy and spiritedness, sexual and creative, of older women, once freed, is powerful enough to present a challenge few men wish to meet. This too has its history. In a study of the persecution of women as witches,[5] Carol Karlsen found that:

> the primary group vulnerable to such accusations was older women between 40 and 60, or women past child-bearing age . . . generally women who were widows or single and who had some reputation as healers or midwives . . . who often had come into some inheritance of land . . . with a reputation for lack of docility: a particular class of women who were dangerous to the normative definitions of woman in society.

These women were stripped of their possessions, discredited, ostracised or put to death. Today things are not all that different. A woman of that age, with ostensible freedom from ties, has to become independent with defiance, in the face of limiting prejudices and the 'invitation to die' which the old receive. She has perforce to be wise enough to come to terms with her deprivations in what purports to be an affluent world. Envy traps her where material and physical concerns dominate. Sexual need has been exaggerated at the expense of the need for physical contact and affection, so sexual hunger and deprivation can be a torment: serpents and memories writhing around her head. This is particularly acute in our time: these women were born in the dark 1930s and 1940s: the optimistic 1950s promised a patriarchal heaven which by the 1980s looks more like hell.

A woman knows intimately when the world's values have gone awry and are heartless and harmful. That knowledge has been silenced and must be reclaimed and given voice if she is to change those values. Medusa in her sad wisdom knows that her capacity to love was abused by the woman-hating god: only by casting off the sick accumulation of feelings and thoughts, the sick persona she has taken on, will she release it and discover what it can do to give meaning to life on earth – for herself and others. The death-dealing male powers who are prepared to risk despoiling or destroying our planet have projected on to mature women, their peers, all their impotence, envy and sterility, having already appropriated their body-life and political power for their own ends. They are not confronting their own climacteric, and our civilisation, as the composer Michael Tippett recently observed, is at a stage of climacteric. In government, a powerful woman such as Margaret Thatcher, unsupported by any kind of feminine culture, is particularly exposed to the danger of being turned into a Medusa in a male-dominated political world.

The older woman easily becomes 'manic-depressive', at times strident, animus-driven, at others hopeless and despondent. Her essential womanhood has become lost to her and turned sour. If she comes to psychotherapy it will be for her the mirror-shield with which her own inner Perseus will confront what she has become. She will need to reject society's projections, resolve to renew her vitality, and work through the transition to an enlightened maturity. Releasing the stuck feelings which have held her fast will get her energy moving. The support of other women and the women's movement will be revitalising. The more drastic surgery, the cutting away from her past, from the expectations and the conditioning that are no longer appropriate and only harm her, will be difficult and painful. Under patriarchy she has not experienced, as she ought to have done in adolescence, the break from the incestuous partnership with her father. At a deep psychic level he still fills her emptiness, wounds her with his personal rejections, and fails to be the spiritual father she needs, transcending the sexual or material father: the Acrisius-Danae relationship – improperly resolved because she is banished from his realm.

Older women today have to accept how that has damaged their lives, and they must 'cut their losses': cut away the Medusa grudge and despondency. For some it is a deeply challenging process, involving a complete revaluation of all they have been, a realisation of how they have become clogged up with the 'penis envy' that patriarchy promotes, names and then derides, and finally the acceptance – constantly resisted – that the absent husband, father or God, in the form she has always known or conceptualised him, is never going to return.[6] The disillusionment is deeply disturbing (the Medusa death) but the shift to another perspective, where the woman rests in her own energy and power, has in it a rightness, a balance, and a liberation of spirit that are truly symbolised by Pegasus.

Though a woman may handle this transition in herself with the support of therapy or of other women, and endure the process as a slow purging, she may well find her Perseus at this time, and this effects a more dramatic healing. She becomes involved with, perhaps falls in love with, a younger man – a colleague, her therapist or doctor, or, less awarely perhaps, her own son. He is her 'lost youth' and through him she hopes to live again. Unconsciously she recalls her young father or husband of thirty or forty years back. What she can learn through this is that he represents part of herself, as yet undeveloped, that she needs to manifest in herself, her 'masculine' creativity, her inner 'divine child' Perseus, the renascent spiritual father-principle who will replace the absent father of her lived experience. In myth he appears traditionally as the son-lover; this whole area is examined extensively by James Hillman (1973).

The younger man – son, lover or friend, helps her through this transition provided he carefully follows Perseus's role, recognises her need for self-realisation and spirituality, and refuses to be devoured by her envious appropriation of his youth or her sexual need. If need be he must cut off contact with what will seem like the cold brutality of the sickle. He will need the mirror-shield to protect him from her despair, anxious distress or frantic behaviour. The Medusa, after a while, can make us feel a guilt which turns us to stone. This guilt-relationship between mother and son also needs to be scrutinised in the mirror. Our younger enlightened men can't be expected to take responsibility for the sins of their fathers the patriarchs. That too is the meaning of Perseus's fathering by Zeus: he need not feel the guilty connectedness to the men whose regime has been so harmful.

The younger man in this relationship is always, at some level, seeking self-realisation through the feminine, looking perhaps for the archetypal lost earth-mother, source of all life, or for moon-consciousness. He may or may not know that he is trying to find the meaning of his life through her. He will be drawn to a mother-figure if, in today's world, he has no father to believe in or wish to emulate. Yet she herself is out of touch with the earth and the moon and cannot give him the spiritual breathing-space he needs. Danae was virtually unmothered: all women suffer from the weakened matriarchal connection, the lack of feminine substance, absent mothering.[7] So between them, they must explore their relationship and its sexual-spiritual component. They both need to arrive at a place beyond incestuous relating and he usually has to wrestle with her to do that. He helps to release that creativity in her which his father's generation stifled, which now threatens him with its stuckness, making him feel stuck also. One such man said of the older woman he had been involved with, partly on the basis of an interest in anti-sexism,

> 'She's so obsessed with her feminism, so militant, so self-centred, she can't see me at all. She wants me to be just like *she* wants the non-sexist man to be. And right now. But no way. I've got to work that out for myself – it's going to take time. I think I'll need a younger woman to work it out with.'

He later found his Andromeda.

Above all he must ensure that she properly mourns the missing father, as he must also, and then brings the mourning to an end. Perseus's cutting gesture is like that of the bereavement counsellor who has to advise the mourner that an ending to grieving must be made. The woman has to accept that this potential 'spiritual father' is of the son generation: she cannot find in him the missing father or husband who would match her maturity. She must find her own inner spirituality, and with it a healthier sexuality than was possible in the fertile years that trapped and enslaved her to body-life. This may mean relating to men in many different ways.[8] As we shall see, the Pegasus imagination, the Andromeda experience, and other aspects of the myth can help her achieve that. Women who do reach this kind of clarity become a source of lively non-pressuring wisdom, free of the tired patronising quality of the male elders of society.

Death and regeneration

When the Medusa's head fell it was from her blood that Pegasus sprang. It is the significance of blood that must be remembered. It was said that subsequently Athena gave that blood to Aesclepios, god of medicine, and it had the capacity either to heal or to kill. Blood-loss marks the biological feminine and is central to all the mystery of woman's life: blood-connections, bleeding and death in menstruation and childbirth. When male-dominated societies lose touch with cyclical menstrual meaning they become bloodthirsty in other ways.[9] The Medusa experience is that of the 'curse' – of pre-menstrual tension (during which many women feel Medusa-like) followed by sudden release, after either the death or the engendering of life in sperm and ovum – represented variously by Medusa's head, Perseus and Pegasus. (See Chapter 12, p. 162.) The end of the menstrual cycle, and the end of menstruation at menopause, marks a transition from childbearing to an expanded creative energy which is spiritual and beyond womb-bound personality.

Thus the myth keeps us in touch with the basic destructive-creative cycles of our lives, and the meaning of generation, the relationship between generations, and of regeneration. It helps us to live with that process and its rhythm, rather than wastefully try to ignore or combat it – as Acrisius did. Men who can relate to women's menstruality and involve themselves in childbirth experiences are coming closer to feminine wisdom, and will, unlike Acrisius, accept the inevitability of death and the limitations of mortal power. They are then able to own the Medusa in themselves and examine how they manifest her destructiveness, her controlling and corrupt power, in their institutions and political settings or, at a personal level, in their many ways of cheapening sex and relationship. Their ego-investment in such ways of being has to be relinquished, beheaded, if they are to find any worthwhile meaning in their personal or public lives. For some men this does happen, and as painfully as for women: often at the menopausal or pre-retirement stage.[10] Many do not survive: male mortality around 60 is high, particularly for those who, all their lives, have been out of touch with their bodies.

The full meaning of the Medusa's death must be grasped. It is a death, leading the way to a transformation, and allowing the myth to have its meaning involves enduring the death of Medusa at the hands of one's internal Perseus. In other words, it expresses and experiences one's bent toward suicide, self-destruction by choice. Many people do in effect if not in reality commit suicide at transitional stages of life, and in particular around the climacteric. They wreck their own careers, abandon their familiar communities to live in totally different environments, or decide to decline into premature decay. Recklessness often takes over – Perseus lashing out in terror – as the only way of dealing with the despair and fear. Suicide, contemplated, attempted, succeeding or failing, real or symbolic, is about the breakdown in the mind-body relationship, and a statement from the soul. It is struggling to stay honoured in the body, but needs to discard the body which seems now to offer no hope of being the right vehicle for its spiritual journey. Medusa

61

longs to love but cannot in her hideous form; doubtless she also longs to die. Perseus releases her.

His role here is therapeutic, akin to that of the therapist who is prepared to be wholly with the suicidal client in the place of despair, neither judging nor rescuing, but acquiescing in the need for self-annihilation, oblivion, as a prelude to rebirth. The therapist facilitates that process in whatever way the other's soul requires, reflecting in the mirror the enormity of what their life has become to them, what needs to be destroyed and cut away. The suicidal person is, as James Hillman points out, 'in the grip of a symbol . . . the soul insists blindly and passionately on its intention . . . The analyst cannot deny this need to die. He will have to go with it. His job is to help the soul on its way' (Hillman, 1976), using the sickle of Hermes, guide of the souls of the dead to the underworld.

To move from the Medusa state to the Pegasus state is total transformation. The sick body, the overfed ego, is no longer the focus of obsession. Flying away, as Perseus and Pegasus do, perhaps shrugging our shoulders with a certain callousness, we leave behind the slumped, diseased and headless body of Medusa on the ground. It is as we imagine the soul perhaps, flying away at death from the body it has inhabited for so long. Looking back at her body may move us to sadness, anger, disappointed yearning, relief, nauseous repulsion. It stirs a memory in us of the discarded placenta from which, when the cord is cut, we free ourselves for entry into new life.

Chapter 7

Pegasus:
The farther reaches of imagination

The moment of Medusa's death and Pegasus's birth is one of acute and dramatic intensity: those who experience it in their lives speak of the extraordinary proximity of black deathliness, deepest existential despair, with ecstatic vitality and radiant hopefulness, as though only when we feel death can we really exquisitely savour life. One person described that moment thus: 'It's as though everything is so bad – really, undeniably, utterly negative, all you can do is flip the coin over and start from the positive side.' A concentration camp survivor spoke of the years following his release as a time of bitter despairing meaninglessness: hatred of life and human beings. Then quite suddenly and involuntarily it switched: to a powerful love of people and a joy in life which informed his new work in healing and rehabilitation. It seemed then that meaning was given to all the agony of suffering and cruelty he had seen and endured.

This is life-renewal: Pegasus is born of the Medusa's blood that both kills and heals. He rises, white and winged, with an uplift, a release, that is breathtaking, shocking, splendid. His qualities of airborne movement, the horse's strength and rhythmic grace, the balancing power of wings (angel's or bird's), the unchecked soaring toward unknown Olympus, all have a power that gradually comes within our confident command as we allow ourselves to trust our bodies, our spirituality, without the control of our minds.

The immediate Pegasus reaction is of release and relief: a sudden change of energy: burdens, depression, constipation, stuckness, seem miraculously to disappear: one is no longer a dying being

64

looking back obsessively on a wasted life, but a living forward-looking being with *élan vital* – seemingly infinite possibilities and directions available: 'the sky's the limit'. Pegasus, so long trapped in Medusa's sick constricted body, emerges with joy, feeling all the new power of expansion, stretching legs and striding off. One woman in a workshop burst spontaneously into wordless song, and spoke of the tremendous physical release that gave her: there was for her, as for many others, a sudden freeing of breathing, a freeing of muscular tightness. People were yawning, stretching, bursting out laughing.

Pegasus was experienced in people's imagination thus:

> Bucking bronco
> born of blood
> borne away
> on beats of wings
> galloping, pulsating, pure
> into cool and clear blue air
> my golden sun brings
> harvest of the sky
> and richer blood
> in hooves, and hind and heart

ecstasy – soaring – belly-laugh – upright – dignity – snort – abandon – power – grace – worth – self-knowledge – strength

> Is this what release is? That now I can look down and question, instead of looking in to question?

> At last! At last! That part of me
> I thought was me is hacked away
> At last the energy has flown out free
> From binding threads of tangled thought
> From past, from future and from what might be.

I soar, I feel the stretch in my belly, the strength in my back and wings. They open wide and clear against my flanks causing the powerful surge toward the heavens. I catch sight of a young man, arms outstretched, calling 'Wait for me'. As he catches my eye he leaps to join me and together we stride the universe.

Sometimes the release of anger is an accompaniment: the life-aggression of the creature determined to get out of the womb, or the anger at the wasted time spent in it. One woman, a nursing sister, spoke of what had happened to her as matron in a private home for the rich mentally ill, where she'd grown increasingly unhappy and 'evil-tempered':

> 'In the end I got so *bored* with being a tragic, miserable, morbid Medusa I wanted to scream. I was alone in my room after a meeting with the board of management and I just started raging and yelling, "I've got to get out of here! This is not what life's about!" And I took off. I walked out of that place and never went back. And afterwards I couldn't imagine how I'd let the director have such a hold on me . . . as though outside his little domain there would be nothing else . . . And I'd turned into an absolute fright there.'

She then wrote the director a letter explaining exactly how he'd abused, controlled and manipulated her creativity and perverted her goodwill. 'I could never have dreamed I'd ever say all that to him.' She had found her voice and her imagination, and thereafter was aware of her own strength: that her values and principles were not to be subordinated to such a man's repressive authoritarian money-making structure. From then on, using her newly freed resourcefulness, she took on a position of authority herself in a health centre and developed a non-hierarchical staff organisation based on co-operative principles. .

The transition involved here – and we can see it in many occurrences in group, family or political life – marks a release from the material greed-and-envy-oriented regime, the addictive profit-making system which becomes a closed-circuit monster paralysing the spirit of those caught in it. Often an older woman within such a system becomes a Medusa, taking the negative projections, scapegoated. From that state the shift is to something which is other-directed, has creative aspirations, spiritual purpose. The original incentive or vision on which the project, or the participants' involvement in it, was based, is born again. The mood is of enlightenment, uplift, release from an unwanted burden.

The same transition is experienced in the release from addictions such as smoking, alcohol, drugs, over- or under-eating. At some point in defeating these there is no alternative to a drastic and painful severance. The reward is a chance to cultivate the spiritual need and aspiration which so often lie behind those addictions, and a new life of the body.[1] All these freedoms are represented by Pegasus, who is health, and health related especially to sexuality and to the lungs and the heart, where our spirituality is active, taking in and sustaining the vital breath of life, and responding to the pulse beat, the rhythms and beauty of the universe.

There is also 'seeing the light' after the darkness of Medusa's cave. Pegasus is often pictured flying toward or alongside the rainbow, symbol of benign spectral light and the bridging of heaven and earth, which replaces overcast cloudy skies. I have found no reference to this in published mythology: it seems to have 'come from nowhere'.

There is a sense of infinite possibilities, expansion, freedom in space and time. This space and time is important, since they are always needed in periods of transition, to allow unconscious and conscious creative development to take place unrestricted: just as we need the space and time to sleep and to rest so that we may dream and reflect on our dreams.

The freeing of individual sexual energy is obviously indicated here also: Pegasus is a horse, a potent sexual symbol, and his release and flight have an orgasmic quality. The frozen, bound or perverted sexuality of the Medusa gives way to a sexuality in which the body is an orgasmic vehicle for transcendence, for the 'little death'. And just as Pegasus is a spirit born into new life, so he may symbolise also the soul released from the body in death. This liberation and expansion of imaginative possibilities can of course be frightening, dizzying: humans fear freedom, orgasm, death. Pegasus is fearless, riding the air.

One woman after attending a workshop had a dream in which she watched a red London double-decker bus soaring through exquisite blue skies toward the rainbow. London buses are notable for their stability and balance. There had been several occasions recently when underground trains had been stuck in tunnels for hours: she'd decided to avoid this nightmare (Medusa cave) possibility and go by bus. Her local bus travelled through a working-class area, and she associated her sexuality and creativity with her working-class background: she had recently given up a constricting 9–5 office job and was aiming to become a freelance full-time dance teacher.

Attempts to identify with Pegasus through movement immediately raise the issue of his ability to fly. Humans can't do that: we can never forget that Pegasus is intrinsically beyond our capacities. Human bodies can only pretend to fly while their feet are on the ground. But in the simulated movement we experience the freeing and exercise of pelvic 'horse' power, of the loins, and a strong rhythmic sense of fantasised leaping, soaring, levelling out, balancing: the exhilarating and reassuring feeling of resting on air-resistance. Many people recall the Pegasus in Walt Disney's film *Fantasia* in whom this kind of movement was vividly conveyed.

Humans, at birth, fall out of the womb into gravity and space: the shock is traumatic: we experience our first fear of falling, of not being contained. Unlike horses we don't then immediately stand on our feet. There is a loss of identity, of ego. Medusa is very much the stuck inflated ego. Any transition in which there is a free-floating lack of definition or identity is threatening for humans in that it calls up the anxieties of ungroundedness at birth. But the elation of breathing for oneself with the power of newborn lungs, instead of 'being breathed', is also there: the Pegasus rhythms, the levitation, the inspiration and aspiration are all vital features of spirituality, the breath of life. To respect that and cultivate it is to be truly creative in the space between earth and heaven.

The difficulties we have in that space, and in those life-transitions which call for a re-assessment of the relationship of body and soul or spirit, such as puberty, orgasm, childbirth, climacteric, are caused by residual, sometimes chronic body tensions which are reinforced by personal and medical attitudes that fail to see that these are times of spiritual crisis, and opportunity for spiritual enlightenment. The more tense, the more held and holding Medusa has been, pinning us to paralytic obsession with our bodies, the more frightening the Pegasus state is by contrast. The healthy release of energetic vibrations in the body is misread as 'there's something wrong with me' – this is akin to the pain we experience when a limb that has 'gone to sleep' comes to life – not a pathological condition but a restoration of free feeling that makes us realise how tense we have been hitherto.

The sad fact about the Medusa is that she has no power of imagination; enclosed in her cave, her eyes and thoughts are narrowly focused: she has lost faith and trust in expansion, and she forgets the spaces outside, forgets that the imagination can be exercised and stretched – just as the limbs can – so that there can be strength and a taking charge of the newly released energy. Pegasus represents exercise.

Erik Erikson, in *Toys and Reasons* (Erikson 1978), writes of the leap:

> Plato . . . sees the model of true playfulness in the need of all young creatures, animal and human, to leap. To truly leap, you must learn how to use the ground as a springboard, and how to land resiliently and safely. It means to test the leeway allowed by given limits; to outdo and yet not escape gravity . . . there is always a surprising element, surpassing mere repetition or habituation, and at its best suggesting some virgin chance conquered, some divine leeway shared.

To leave the Medusa state is often to take a leap in the dark: it requires Perseus's courage – foolhardiness? (The Tarot Fool, symbol of death and rebirth, is seen cheerfully stepping off the edge of a cliff.) But we can remind ourselves of Pegasus's buoyancy and elation – and for many this is a release into laughter also, distancing ourselves from the self-important solemnity of Medusa's cave, enjoying the (sometimes sick) joke of the perversity of human behaviour, perhaps snorting and farting like Pegasus, relaxing, letting go to our animal nature with irreverent lightness. The interplay of gravity and levity are Pegasus's concerns, in both a physical and an emotional sense.

Pegasus is the offspring of Poseidon, a 'lower god' who is reputed to have created the horse, and of Medusa, a human, possibly a priestess. Pegasus's energy is both less and more than human: animal and divine. In the legends there are suggestions about the problems in harnessing that energy. In some versions of the story Perseus rides away on his back for a while, thereby escaping the pursuing Gorgon sisters, before taking off with his own winged feet: it is as though Pegasus launches Perseus, initiates him into his male sexuality. The intimate sexual connection between horse and horse-rider (portrayed strikingly by Tolstoy in *Anna Karenina* and D. H. Lawrence in *St Mawr* and *Women in Love*) is suggested here. In some versions Chrysaor, the 'golden warrior' is born along with Pegasus as the horse's accompanying rider. Later Bellerophon attempts to ride him but is shaken off and, hurt by the fall, limps in melancholy through life thereafter. Since he is a bellicose individual we may suppose there was a power-struggle with the horse, and

Bellerophon had to learn the limits of human control over such power as Pegasus has: we subjugate our sexuality at our peril, and must learn to respect its power.

Pegasus flies on his own without mortal riders. Yet voluntarily he works for Zeus, delivering the god's thunderbolts, and he serves the Muses, scraping the ground with his foot so that a stream flows from which they drink. And they care for him: he is docile and quiescent in their presence. The power of the sexual, of our animal nature, our imaginative power also, can be canalised into the arts, which 'tame' it with love and respectful mutuality, not seeking to suppress or overly control it, but help it find significant form.

The 'taming' is often needed. Pegasus, unreined, can be dangerous: free ungrounded fantasy approaches the borders of psychosis. Individuals with genius are always close to madness and need society's understanding to help them hold on to sanity. And in group as in individual life we see the pitfalls of 'unbridled' sexuality, wilfulness and narcissism in the liberated, the inflation or the ungrounded other-worldliness or unrealism of spiritual, or political movements. All these are Pegasus untamed, anarchical, and needing harnessing, containment in form. Other-worldly spiritual movements need to find meaning through willing service (not subservience) to Zeus or the Muses: to some purpose or ideal, religious or aesthetic, which in its turn relates back to humanity, to ground, to earth-bound people.

So the imaginative Pegasus flight is one thing: Perseus's need to come down to earth is another. This was a crucial realisation for one man who made these notes in a workshop:

> 'Yes I feel like Pegasus right now – jumpy – expansive – I'm waiting to move to a bigger house – I've got these marvellous plans for how it's going to be. But I can't get there: the solicitors and bank managers and surveyors are dragging their feet. And I'm looking down on those little people in their offices, from my splendid wide-open heights. Don't they understand I've got these wonderful ideas for our new home, my future? How dare they control me with their pettiness. I want to kick them off . . . but that wouldn't help. My wife actually said "You'll have to hold your horses for a while"!'

He observed some weeks later, soberly, after some feelings of anti-climax in his new environment, that he was beginning to see that there were two kinds of coming down to earth: landing, arriving where you need to be, to be who you are, in the place that's at last yours, landing on your feet; but also coming down to earth in the place that's *theirs*: the reality of what it's like in this world, even when you have your new home.

Pegasus lands on his feet with the Muses, but Perseus will have to land on dangerous mortal territory. The duality is always there: we find our truth, the ideal, fantasised forms of our imagining that are the Muses' domain; and still we must live in the real world of our limited human capacities and our interdependence with difficult other persons and corrupt powers. It is the duality of innocence and experience that William Blake was aware of. Each time we are born anew with Pegasus our innocent soul with its tremendous spiritual-sexual energy comes again into a world which has not changed as we have (– even though our new perception of it does in some measure change it for us). We leave the Medusa's womb but now have to relate to a 'mother' and 'family', an environment, which will be represented by Cassiopaeia's kingdom, whom experience may have made corrupt and cynical. Our fear of freedom, and of the backlash that it may attract, can paralyse us. But as all famous heroes report, bravery is spurred on by, and achieved in spite of, terror: they are not fearless. Certainly Perseus is no hardened warrior: he runs away from the Gorgons: he is the epitome of inexperience.

And he is about to face something worse than the Medusa. But the difference is that it will no longer be just the personal threat to his individual life that is involved: it is the threat to another person – to his 'other half' Andromeda. This calls up his bravery and makes him more than the half-person he was. Our spirituality and self-realisation are not only a question of the mind's and the heart's need for transcendence and imaginative Pegasus expansion: they involve the mind and the heart's reaching out to humanity, feeling, suffering alongside us, in mutuality, suffering the unideal existence of human beings in their present stage of evolution.

Beyond stress: the evolutionary leap

Pegasus is certainly about evolutionary development and the imagined transcendence of what seem to be human limitations. He goes with the freeing of mind, the shift from old concepts or constructs, sets, fixed ideas, constricting forms, inflexible theories or linguistic structures.[2] The paradigm shift, the change of perspective or premise is an escape from a Medusa rigidity that has seemed incontrovertible. Dorothy Rowe, in her book on depression, portrays it as locked in by unshifting constructs of reality (Rowe 1983). John Layard called it 'withheld knowledge'.[3] The Medusa (like the term 'depression' itself) is a left-brain, male-orientated concept or construct: defined, confined by the logos mentality of Athena and Polydectes, 'mentality' which must know, and have power through knowledge – or the withholding of knowledge. But Medusa's inner truth, her imagination, right-brain intuition, her 'unknowing', is as wordless as Pegasus, and as boundless in its freedom to fly, once she lets it go.

There are things we do not know which are 'beyond our ken', that our imagination has some idea of, but cannot, should not, attempt to firm up by premature articulation, Bellerophon control, in the anarchical stage of transition after we are freed from old forms, concepts, languages. We have to experiment for some time with sounds and silences before finding a new language. For the feminine, for women at present this is undoubtedly so, as they struggle to express truths for which patriarchy has no words.

Pegasus's relationship with the Muses suggests that only the artistic creative and flexible right-brain modes of expression, many of them non-verbal, like music, mime, art, can foster human personal and transpersonal potential and the evolutionary process which of its nature cannot possibly be 'known'. Pegasus is about the development of the human animal and its relation to the human capacity to think, and to make images and symbols: in other words, the 'old brain' and its relation to the 'new brain'. This symbol, Pegasus itself, is usually referred to as 'he', but there is no reason to accept that: Pegasus combines 'feminine' and 'masculine' attributes and may be androgynous: certainly beyond concepts of male/female or of bisexuality, being simply itself, Pegasus and indefinable in human terms.

To that extent we recognise Pegasus's existence outside our norms of space and time: this is the fourth-dimension experience. It is the area of Einsteinian relativity (Blake's description of the 'single vision' of Newtonian physics relates to the fixed stare Medusa qualities) and of the 'Tao of physics', where science and religion seem now to be meeting.[4] That is a 'new paradigm' place and the place of the 'quantum leap'. In brain evolution such leaps happen, at moments of intense stress, in 'peripheral isolates' – which could well describe Danae, Perseus and Medusa, as it does all creative persons who are outcasts. To quote Marilyn Ferguson:

> *Punctuationalism* or *punctuated equilibrium* suggests that the equilibrium of life is 'punctuated' from time to time by severe stress. If a small segment of the ancestral population is isolated at the periphery of its accustomed range, it may give way to a new species. Also, *the population is stressed intensely because it is living at the edge of its tolerance* . . . 'Small peripheral isolates are the laboratory of evolutionary change'.
>
> The new paradigm attributes evolution to periodic leaps by small groups (Ferguson 1982).

Pegasus, combining the animality of the old brain and the imagined boundless potential of the new brain, suggests such a leap. The remainder of the myth offers an imagined result of such a leap: a new code whose key is the Medusa head, a new dynasty, and finally a new species of woman in Gorgophone. Is it fanciful to suggest that the evolutionary leap now is from the concept of 'homo sapiens' to that of 'mulier sapientia'?

The interim place, beyond space and time, in which Pegasus exists, has a schizoid quality about it, a strength of independence, science, of a rarefied, distilled spirituality and relativistic detachment such as one associates with physicists like Einstein. Its 'masculinity' contrasts with – and complements – the polluted, corruptible feminine body, the earth-bound, creative, feeling, spirituality of Medusa. Perhaps that is why we tend to think of Pegasus as male: the energy that thrusts its way through and out of the clammy confines of the flesh. Yet the schizoid scientific position is, in modern physics, the basis for a right-brain activity akin to poetic organisation. As people ripen into old age they become more androgynous.

Paradox and the swinging between concepts, the dissolution of fixed polarities, is inherent to this place. Pegasus, being an animal, suggests that in our own evolutionary process there may have to be a sort of regression to the animal, the old brain in us, if we are to become 'winged' – more than earthbound creatures: as though we have to undo for a while, unlearn the way we have learned to walk upright on the earth. Insofar as that mortal way may have denied our animal capacities and strengths and animal relatedness to natural process, our ecological selves (the old brain connects us to the earth, the earth-goddess) then those strengths must be regained by shedding for a while the old structures, ways of walking or, with Medusa, staying inert. The ecological movements are indeed aiming to restore that primal sense of the inter-connectedness of all elements of nature, calling up in us both the humility and the trust in our inner powers that animals have, which our culture has largely robbed us of.[5]

In personal development, in therapy, the Pegasus state is often in fact marked by a regression to a pre-walking stage. The walking learned in infancy, usually at the same time as toilet-training, rigidifies the legs, locking the knees and the lower back, so that pelvic activity is tightly controlled and there is not the motility, the comfortable relationship to the ground, the body flexibility, that animals have. Shedding this complex, the paralysing super-ego that limits our sexuality, creativity and spiritual imagination and ungrounds us, means unlearning and re-learning how to walk (see chapter 12).

At the same time, we want to be free as birds. Somewhere in evolution, the four-legged creature looked up perhaps at the birds and longed to fly, so he got on to two feet to be upright, aspiring upwards. To cope with the fact of his heaviness, gravity, standing on earth, and his vulnerability, soft breast and heart bared to all comers, and the dangerous treacherousness of his desire to fly, his knowledge of mortality, he created a complex set of tensions and controls over his body, feelings and imaginings. And we have made machines so that we may fly, and these very machines and their uses are the mark of our limitations and misunderstandings. Our wings are not in right relationship yet with our human powers on earth. Perhaps they are destined to take us away from this planet, which looks like being on the verge of death, so that we settle on another. Thus the Pegasus transition state is of crucial importance to our consciousness at present.

We are made such that we constantly strive to transcend what we are, perhaps into a state where we do not have to know a meaning. Pegasus doesn't think about flying: he flies. Striving for logical meaning with our minds invites madness and disorientation. The word is interesting, for the mysticism and relative ego-lessness of the oriental way of life can better carry and submit to not understanding than can the western. Their meditation practices ground them even as they allow the spirit to enter, and transcendence to be experienced (von Dürkheim 1956).

The condition of unknowing, so hard for westerners to accept, the Tao place of wordlessness, the 'still point of the turning world', where the only concept is that there are no concepts, is where we feel most at harmony with ourselves and the universe, feel 'in love'. Around the inner still point is the outer movement, the cosmic dance, which is its own wisdom. We tap only rarely into this awareness, calling it eternity, the collective unconscious, implicate order, astral plane, ecstasy, receiving intimations of it through mystic experiences, dreams, synchronicities, drugs. And the self-unconsciousness and humility required to be more often in that place are exactly what animals have, as poets like D. H. Lawrence and Walt Whitman appreciated:

> I think I could turn and live with animals, they are so placid and
> self-contained,
> I stand and look at them long and long.
> They do not sweat and whine about their condition,
> They do not lie awake in the dark and weep for their sins,
> Not one is dissatisfied, not one is demented with the mania of
> owning things,
> Not one kneels to another, nor to his kind that lived thousands
> of years ago,
> Not one is respectable or unhappy over the whole earth.
> (Whitman)

So the myth reminds us, through an animal, that part of our potential for love and meaningful living lies in the humility of abdicating superconscious control.

Watching Pegasus, riding on him, Perseus must feel that soaring yet balanced sense of unbounded potential. What could we human beings only do, with our amazing resources of imagination, energy and daring, our symbolising minds? We still have difficulty harnessing and organising that energy, understanding how best to use such powers to save our world from slow or violent destruction, the Medusa, or Poseidon's monster, that threaten us. We have visions of what might be, and our cynicism, our laziness, born of depression, reduces those visions to fantasies. Perseus is innocent enough and fatherless enough to be free of the cynicism and depression of the patriarchs. His saving of Andromeda and his marriage to her are not romantic fantasy but a vision which is made to work.

> 'I know exactly how Perseus feels,' said one man. 'When I've been to a "New Age" conference in the country somewhere and we've had this marvellous experience of a positive, hopeful consciousness, a sense of the immense potential for transformation in each one of us, that could do such wonderful things for the world (and we aren't by any means starry-eyed): that's Pegasus, that's health. Then I go back to London and all I see is pollution – dirt and depression and sickness and pettiness and materialism, and I wonder how on earth all that inspiration and hopefulness I had is going to survive? That's like being confronted with Andromeda on the rock. Having to deal with the monster, and the parents that called up the monster . . .'

So Perseus may keep Pegasus as a reminder, as the symbol he is, of expansive imagination, of freedom and balance, the bridging of earth and heaven, aspiration, infinity. Meanwhile he must find his way on earth, find a home, learn what being a man means in the world. He has slain the Medusa, and is no longer held back by the mother who has bound his sexuality and his freedom to be: nor is he at the mercy of the treacherous step-father Polydectes. He has a new autonomy, and must develop inner authority to guide him in the dangerous world he has now been cast into. The next series of events mark vital points of growth: the story is simple but precise and pertinent, and it can serve as a paradigm and a guide for the handling of situations of great complexity.

Chapter 8

Perseus and Andromeda:
Helplessness and salvation of the feminine

Perseus flies onward with winged feet: he sees a beautiful naked young woman chained to a rock and immediately falls in love with her. Our reaction to that, before we know any of the detail of what, where or how, is immediate: we expect a romantic outcome, a solution, a happy ending, or we hope for it, and will feel tragic disappointment should it not happen. In fact, Perseus and Andromeda have to deal with many complications, but for them and us the need is undoubtedly to fulfil that simple concept of union, so often generated by the act of 'falling in love'.

Bion group dynamic theory speaks of the fantasy by a threatened group that it will be saved by a pairing of two of its members – clearly related to survival needs, for the continuation of the species, reproduction. Certainly this fantasy is exploited by forces that wish to divert attention from threat: newspapers will suddenly concentrate on a love story, or governments mount a royal wedding, at times of economic or political distress. The underlying psychic need, however, for real or symbolic union does have to be met: the need is the greater at times of disunion, of warlike tension, of deprivation and the rule of hatred. In some sense the threatened community will indeed be 'saved' by this image of pairing. Romantic love has an essential element of idealism, which can co-exist with and underpin realism, disillusionment, and mature relationship.

The psychic need is to achieve a 'bisexual' harmony of our right and left brain, essential to creativity: Eastern philosophy and Jungian psychology are much concerned with this. At another level

there is the psychological need – explored particularly by Freudians – to heal and resolve the guilt we experience (much accentuated when the 'time is out of joint') at having split our parents, kept them apart, thereby keeping ourselves from being whole. When, in psychotherapy, we 'allow the parents to come together', we validate our own conceived existence, and become more 'together' ourselves. Perseus, in search of identity, has to put himself together.

Most people meet these needs by setting up their own pairings. By finding our own mate, instituting a new marriage, we release our parents and ourselves from the domination of their old marriage over us. If Perseus is confused about his parentage, about his killing of the Medusa, then loving and marrying Andromeda helps to heal the disintegrating splits within him. And he does 'revise', even as he recalls, the circumstances of his own birth. He, like Zeus his father, flies in, on divine wings, to the helpless mortal girl. But the situation is different in significant respects: not enclosed but public and open, to be resolved in human and realistic terms; not a clandestine impregnation and departure of the father but a prelude to marriage, to commitment and fatherhood; and Andromeda has a very different psychological make-up from Danae. In confronting and separating herself from her parents she is the 'new' self-directed woman. In our time, born, like Perseus, in the optimistic, enlightened 1950s and 1960s, yet growing up under the shadow of impending world disaster, she has perforce a realism and courage and energy that is less depressed, clearer than that of the mother and grandmother. Certainly there has been a welcome increase of clarity in that generation's attitude to marriage.

These are the details of Andromeda's story: her parents are Cepheus and Cassiopeia, King and Queen of Joppa in Philistia. Cassiopeia boasted that she and her daughter were more beautiful that the Nereids, the sea-nymphs. They immediately complained to their protector Poseidon, who unleashed a horrifying female sea-monster which ravaged great expanses of nearby land. He threatened to devastate their entire kingdom unless a sacrifice were offered: the citizens insisted the royal princess be offered up to the monster. When Perseus sees her plight he asks her parents if he can marry her if he saves her from death: they agree. He slays the monster – some say with a sword, as he flies down from above, others, by holding up the Medusa's head to kill it. When he claims Andromeda for his bride, her parents refuse and bring to their palace numbers of other more prosperous or attractive suitors. These Perseus disposes of with the Medusa's head. Andromeda insists on marrying Perseus and her parents have to agree to the match: the wedded couple subsequently leave for Seriphos to rejoin Danae and deal with Polydectes.

This marriage, of the spiritually inspired young man who has broken free from egotistical patriarchy and maternal domination, and the incorruptible young woman who has defied, and escaped from, parental materialism and possessiveness, is an important and healthy one, both personally and symbolically. The healing resolution of male/female mutual wounding through generational development, where the children achieve a union the parents could not attain, is one we see often in literature. Shakespeare addresses the theme time and again: *Romeo and Juliet* is where he begins to explore it in earnest: *Hamlet* marks his inability to achieve the resolution. *The Tempest* is where it is finally reached – and it involves the patriarch giving up his power. Emily Brontë's *Wuthering Heights* has a similar two-generation pattern. D. H. Lawrence, in the sequence of *The Rainbow* and *Women in Love*, goes through the same process.

All these works are attempting to heal the split between men and women, masculine and feminine, that has been causing more and more damage as centuries of western civilisation go by. To effect that coming together today, the healing of personal relationships, against a background of painful disruption, of divorce and family disintegration, is very difficult. The sort of simple love relationship that happens between Perseus and Andromeda can be killed by cynicism, interference, envy, pessimism, before it even has a chance to develop and discover what it is. This destructive illwill, personified in Andromeda's parents, has to be counteracted: some sort of blessing is needed for a marriage to flourish. Perseus, using the Medusa head, proof of his capacity to demolish the envy that might have made him impotent, does counteract it in killing the usurping suitors.

We need to trust that whatever difficulties men and women are experiencing in their relationships at present it is possible to allow love to happen, grow, and form the basis of a healthier regime. Thoughtfulness, constructive thought, is definitely heart-related. There are signs that many thinking men are wanting to heal the wounds inflicted on women. In his book *The Horned God*, which is unusual in its honest grappling with the situation, John Rowan looks at the possibilities for individuals, couples, and groups of men, and sees both difficulty and hope (Rowan 1987). Women too are wanting to heal men who have suffered from the corruption of the feminine principle and from paternal weakness (Starhawk 1979). In a dream workshop recently an anonymous woman's dream was reported by an analyst: 'In my dream I have a twin brother and he has a brain disease. I look at him in distress, and then think, if he has it, I must have it too. We'll share it together.' This kind of equality is suggested in the relationship of Perseus and Andromeda, for she insists on keeping her allegiance with him in his isolated and exposed position, his dis-ease in the regime of her family.

I need to say here that to speak of bisexual or heterosexual creativity is in no way to condemn or undervalue homosexual relationships. They are often based on, and nourish, a love and creativity that needs no apology or justification. In that two-ness a need for an embracing union with 'the other' is being met — provided it is the creative union of separate entities, not a destructive merging and submerging.

The balancing of opposites, the harmonious relationship of Yin and Yang, is what we seek, consciously and unconsciously. On the interplay of doing and being, of control and surrender, of other polarised energies, will depend the progress of any two-person relationship: we shall see that many such features of the relationship between Perseus and Andromeda are suggested by the myth. Jungian psychology is much concerned with this balancing of feminine and masculine within the individual, and sees imbalance in two-person relationships as caused by undue dependence on some needed aspect of the other person, blocking our capacity to manifest it in ourselves. A partnership between a man and a woman is an opportunity for individual growth in two persons, and a dramatisation of their separate modes of growth when they come together.[1]

The threatening monster

The rescue has more than just a romantic meaning. In some ways Perseus and Andromeda represent the mind/body polarity, a common masculine/feminine one. Andromeda is the virgin body, pure and unadulterated and beautiful in its nakedness, much as a newborn's body is. To care for the body, preserve its health, protect it from greed, vain perversion, pollution, addiction, violation, is a task for anyone who 'puts their mind to it'. This Perseus does. Having slain the sick-bodied Medusa, he is able to see clearly the healthy-bodied Andromeda: he will not project negative feelings on to her. Appreciating her beauty, he is impelled to destroy the monster that threatens her. He evinces the positive, careful attitude to the body that marks the healthy person and the prophylactic healer.

Poseidon's monster, the dread shadow called up by Cassiopeia's vanity, manifests today in the poison and destruction brought upon us because of the greed of rampant technological progress: the many industries which pollute the environment or promote unhealth: the cigarette manufacturers, heroin dealers, cosmetic surgeons, arms dealers, chemical drug manufacturers who have an investment in abusing or exploiting people's bodies. The female sea-monster is the dark feminine actively stirred up and unleashed (in contrast to the Medusa, who is rejected, scapegoated and stuck). Poseidon, this 'lower' god, lets loose, unchecked, the violent dark devouring destructiveness of the feminine, the Kali and Lilith qualities, that exploitative men arouse and use with ruthlessness or thoughtlessness, abandoning all fatherly care. This oceanic monster is what ecological disasters are made of, for the subterranean powers of our earth will have their revenge on us if we use or abuse them recklessly, and deny their essential mystery, as Cassiopeia did. The misuse of the earth's mineral resources by industry rebounds on us with a vengeance.

Perseus, the son of a 'higher' god, appreciates the essential spiritual beauty of the body, of Andromeda's body. She now, awaiting Poseidon's revenge, has become the symbol of human beauty, attached to the rock, inseparable from the upper earth's beauty, appealing to be preserved.[2]

The plague of AIDS, and its associated plague of addictive drug-taking, is also Poseidon's monster: promiscuity and greed gone beyond control and threatening to overwhelm us. Many people react as the Philistines did and look for cosmetic solutions and scapegoats, content to ostracise and abandon helpless victims, like Andromeda, to the scourge. The more responsible, like Perseus, meet the hysteria with compassion and the conviction that this monstrous affliction can be dealt with by the restoration of self-respect and meaningful living to a sick society.

We have already seen that mind can only be in right relationship with body through spirit, breathing. Heart and lungs are between head and belly: the channel must be free. The release of Pegasus marked that freeing of breath, of spirit in Perseus, as at birth. Now he needs, as at birth, to connect with another human being who will pace the rhythm and pulsebeat and respond with heartfelt loving and physical warmth: then the spiritual qualities, the love, will thrive. This is the partnership with Andromeda. That caring partnership, between men and women, mind and body, humans and planet earth, saves us from destruction by powers that devour indiscriminately.

Possession and dispossession

Cassiopeia's vanity and irreverence has called up Poseidon's monstrous attack to avenge his protégés. The king's most precious possession is offered as appeasement. When we look at the issues of ownership involved here we see that there are significant messages about the possession of earth and of bodies, issues of territory, of our need for and rights to attachment to land, home, family. Sexuality, dynasty, society are interwoven preoccupations.

The fatherless, homeless Perseus, who cannot know whether he might rule in Seriphos or Argos, flying in whatever direction his winged feet take him, impelled by his newly released sexuality, sees a possible partner and sets about achieving a union. The aimless youth recognises something to hold on to, a woman to whom he can relate. She comes from a 'normal' conventional family, living on its own territory: something he has never experienced. If, as people from 'broken homes' often do, he idealises the family which he assumes, though just now in crisis, to be enviably 'together', he will soon be disillusioned by the parents' infidelity, betrayal, and possessiveness. He is learning about possession. His relationship to Andromeda has a romantic quality, a vital component of innocence and vulnerability in both of them: it has too a realism, and the pain of Andromeda's experience as a victim. This gives her strength and wisdom. He is displaced, dispossessed. Though aware that by

83

patriarchal right, territory is his concern, he is still open to learning about the nature of earth, ground, of what or whom he becomes the owner. He is free of the corruptive pride of the powerful possessor-by-right, the imperialist, the Acrisius or Polydectes. He slays a monster who conquers and devastates earth, and marries a woman who has earth qualities which help ground and strengthen his character and inner authority (he has yet to 'author' a dynasty). He is interested in quality, not quantity, and does not want domination.

Perseus's dispossessed state is significant, suggesting the sort of opportunity given to those who lose empires and must therefore concentrate on and care for local resources and needs: a total revaluation of concern, very much in line with ecological thought and the concept of 'small is beautiful'. The myth at this point is, indeed, saying, back to roots (an earlier civilisation), back to bare truths, humble origins, basic and simple human needs for survival and happiness. The message needs to be taken by the British who, having lost their empire, need to return to the roots of the English-speaking culture that has such great potential for civilisation.[3]

Redemption of the feminine in twentieth-century religion

It is striking that in the literary instances of redemptive 'pairing' I have mentioned – by Shakespeare, Emily Brontë and D. H. Lawrence – the men have all been, like Perseus, dispossessed of the customary appurtenances of male authority: territory, princedom, riches; and the women have all been, like Andromeda, abused, violated or possessed in some way and have survived. Healing and redemption come through this combination. Another interesting example of this leads us in a roundabout way to see how this myth foreshadows the development of the relationship between Christianity and Judaism. In D. M. Thomas's *White Hotel*, the redemptive healing vision which ends the novel (which is so much concerned with corruption of male-female relationships in our century, and Christian-Jewish conflict) is centred on a similar pair of lovers: the one-armed Christian English lieutenant, and the half Jewish woman who has been raped and destroyed by the Nazis. They come together and dedicate themselves to healing and rehabilitation after the horrors of the war. This echoes, in a curious way, our myth. Perseus has similarities with Christ, Andromeda is a princess of Joppa, Jaffa in Palestine, and distinctly semitic. Robert Graves connects her with goddess figures such as Astarte and Ishtar who were later incorporated into unofficial Hebrew deities. If Christianity goes back to its roots it finds the 'Hebrew goddess'.[4] Andromeda's role as scapegoat, victim, and her relations with her bourgeois materialistic parents have a familiar Jewish ring about them. But she is strong, simple, earth-connected, a princess who refuses to be the 'Princess' archetype, apple of the Jewish father's eye and only interested in successful rich men.[5]

The recovery of the pre-Christian goddess archetype, the need to marry the Christ-figure to a strengthening sexual consort can be seen in such works as *The Wild Girl* by Michele Roberts and *The Mists of Avalon* by Marion Bradley. This 'sacred marriage' or *hieros gamos* has a long, archetypal history in myth and in alchemy.[6] The possibility of spiritual revival within the Judaeo-Christian tradition through the redemption, the 'rescue', and recovery of the feminine are suggested by the situation of Perseus and Andromeda. Christianity has indeed lost its authority: God the father is absent, and Christ, like Perseus, the spiritual son, is dispossessed of that popular power the religion once had. Judaism like Andromeda has been abused and violated as a religion, and through the massacre of its people: it could easily succumb to territorial devastation in Israel or soulless, addictive materialism in the diaspora. Whatever reconciliation can be achieved between Christians and Jews would give new meaning to their spirituality, for their separation marks a grievous split in the western psyche and the guilt, the fact of the holocaust, is a wound whose symbolic healing would do much for humankind. To heal the split between masculine and feminine involves the reconciliation of polarised schizoid and hysteric tendencies.[7] Communication needs restoring between the 'absent' schizoid male and the frantic hurting female, between the remote withdrawn spirituality of Christianity and the anxious spiritual enclosedness of Judaism.

Andromeda's naked helplessness

In one modern version improvised in a workshop Andromeda's mother had sold nude photos of her beautiful daughter to a Hugh

Hefner-like entrepreneur who then sought to blackmail her, and take her into high-class prostitution. Her utter helplessness, exposed, sold and betrayed by her parents, was devastating; at the root of it was her inability to counter the exploitative and salacious attitude to her body of the man who threatened her, for there was no way she could make him value it without possessing it. She recognised that she herself found it hard to be naked and unashamed (to allow the photos to be published and not give into the blackmail) and the issue of shame came up as an important factor. For shame and modesty are close: so she was ashamed of her parents' lack of respect and decorum, respect for her privacy. But shame also can be felt as a fear of one's own ugliness: we may be ashamed if our bodies are not loved, and suspect that there is something wrong with us.[8] This is a common experience for the newborn baby, for women, and for anyone who is much deprived of love. In their lonely state they may project their fear and anger with the missing lover or mother, out on to a greedy monster, who wants to swallow them whole, not wishing to savour or taste what must be their badness – a familiar mechanism of paranoia. But behind it lies perhaps the primitive fear that the weak or ugly one, if recognised as such, will be discarded and left to die or, as with some species, actually devoured by the mother.[9] Whenever life is cheap, the body undervalued, then the indiscriminate sacrifice or massacre of lives goes on. All this, in her time on the rock, Andromeda is aware of, and powerless to alter. One woman said, 'I'm shit-scared – and if I shit I really will be an unattractive bad mess, won't I?'

Many people were acutely in touch with Andromeda's experience at the time of the US raids on Libya and the Chernobyl disaster in 1986. One man in a group about this time wept as he talked of his utter despair that he was powerless to do anything to stop what could easily be the horrible, meaningless destruction of all he knew and loved. 'Am I worth nothing?' he asked helplessly. In the group we were able to share the terror that gripped us all, threatening to paralyse us altogether.

The myth makes it clear that it is precisely from that condition of naked despairing helplessness that the appeal must come, to call up the Perseus in the powerful forces that take over our lives, the Perseus within us, who must love us and find resources to save us, restore our humanity and sense of self-worth. And the more we unashamedly expose our fear and our nakedness and our desire for life and love, the more hope there is for salvation.[10] D. H. Lawrence's poem, 'Moral Clothing', is particularly relevant, for he knows that nakedness shows our ugliness as well as our beauty and we must confront each other in a wholeness which is beyond shame:

> When I am clothed I am a moral man,
> and unclothed, the word has no meaning for me.
>
> When I put on my coat, my coat has pockets . . .
>
> When I stand in my shift I have no pockets
> therefore no morality of pockets;
> but still my nakedness is clothed with responsibility
> towards those near and dear to me, my very next of kin.
> I am not yet alone.
>
> Only when I am stripped stark naked I am alone
> and without morals, and without immorality.
> The invisible gods have no moral truck with us.
>
> And if stark naked I approach a fellow-man or fellow-woman
> they must be naked too
> and one of us must expect morality of each other:
> I am that I am, take it or leave it.
> Offer me nothing but that which you are, stark and strange.
> Let there be no accommodation at this issue.

'My nakedness is clothed with responsibilty' – responsibility is what manifests in Andromeda's uniting with Perseus. Though helpless, fragile, physically smaller than the male, Andromeda is vital to his creativity, and has strength and wisdom if she is prepared to use it and he is prepared to recognise and allow it.

Andromeda is naked except for some jewels, and these pose questions. Are they adornments, cosmetic, Cassiopeia's jewels, tokens of worldly riches being sacrificed, perhaps meant to appease the god? Are they symbols of the treasure of her sexuality? Her menstrual blood? Or do they represent craft: the moulding of earth's minerals into aesthetic form, which enhances the human form? The myth leaves it to us to value them as we will, but it surely makes us question their material or symbolic value when they are attached to one who is about to die. For one woman, a teacher, who had suffered much personal, career and political disappointment, Andromeda's jewels gave meaning:

> 'I'm desolate, hopeless. I've spent all my strength trying to
> struggle out of these chains. I can't. I'm terrified: I don't want the
> pain of a horrible death. But I'm resigned now to my fate, I've
> given up struggling, and I can accept this had to be, in the course
> of things. It's fated. These jewels matter: they give me dignity:
> they tell me, and they tell Poseidon, that there can be beauty,
> that human beings can achieve fineness – make something
> beautiful out of the clay of our existence, the earth . . . at this
> moment that seems to matter more than anything else.'

Perseus and Andromeda: the creative interplay of energies

Andromeda's salvation is only the beginning of her emergence from the emotional chains that bound her to her parents. She has the strength – perhaps as a result of her ordeal – to insist on marrying the man who has loved her for her naked self. She gives Perseus respect, honouring him with her trust. In all this she lives up to her name which means 'a leader of men', for she teaches him a way of mature love and gives him the opportunity to establish his potency and grow in their relationship, not allowing interference from the elders.

The myth handles their sexual interplay delicately, and is sensitive to those issues of male and female potency which are always with us, be it in our intimate physical relating or on the wider arena of sexual politics. 'Liberated' women, with their powerful and more wholly encompassing sexuality and creativity, have to learn how to use it wisely to allow men the full potential and potency which can match it. Women may lead, but need to take care not to disempower thereby – which would simply be doing what has been done to them. The handling of weakness and strength, male and female, to find a rhythm which releases the essential energy of both, without either of them having to suppress that energy more or less violently, is the task. Andromeda is both assertive and humble, aware of her weakness but not trading on it as a pathetic victim. She trustfully respects the strength of the man who can give her new life and release her sexuality. She has none of the debilitating negativity, the exhausted or perverted creativity, the aggressive envy of the older generation of women represented by Danae, Medusa and Cassiopeia, who could easily devour, castrate or kill Perseus.

Perseus, for his part, brings the masculine thrust and determination needed to help her, becomes an organiser, negotiator, resourceful, quick-thinking, having a job to do, not concerned with a display of heroics, if anything quite puzzled as to how to proceed. He can be quick to destroy where severance, severity are needed, but he is committed to using his skill and strength in the service of his heart's purpose: the tenderness he feels towards Andromeda, which her vulnerability calls up in him, reminding him undoubtedly of his own, for he is at this moment without support, protection or guidance from any father or family in the face of the dangers of this threatened territory and its regime.

Perseus's action comes from a generosity which is lacking in Andromeda's parents. Generosity is a quality that is of particular significance in men: the root meaning of the word suggests its creative purpose. A generous father gives what he will to his children as a conscious act: their mother's giving is more involuntary from the beginning. Of course it is a question of degree, but in a society where men do most of the possessing their generosity or meanness is an important issue. Withdrawal, refusal to give money, or sex, is a male counterpart to the female who gives, or gives in, with illwill. (Scrooge is a male archetype, the witch with the poisoned apple female.) Perseus exercises a generosity he has perhaps learned from Polydectes, but it does not turn into Polydectes's conditional patronising and blackmailing: Andromeda gives herself to Perseus of her own choice . . . and with goodwill.

Their relationship can serve as a paradigm for what can be achieved when a man and a women give one another mutual support, strengthen each other for positive ends, playing no games of dominance and submission, acknowledging their weaknesses and strengths and not exploiting them in competitiveness.

If this beginning relationship gets off to a promising start in this way that doesn't mean it is going to be easy. Difficulty is always there. Insofar as Perseus and Andromeda have been sheltered, their lives protected and easy, so they will have to grapple with difficulty and toughen themselves for it, without the heroic stance which is usually blind to the real challenges. The precious life of the prince and princess cannot be maintained as a defence against the arduous tasks, the hard work of making something new out of the debris of the old. That is where 'willpower' in its best sense must come in.

Love and Will are sometimes seen as aspects of the feminine/ masculine polarity. Perseus certainly exemplifies 'where there's a will there's a way', bringing order to the chaotic situation that results from unrestricted feminine impulses abused or running riot, the love principle seduced and gone astray. Andromeda represents Love in her fidelity to Perseus – and also in her role of sacrifice; willing or not, she is laying down her life for the sake of her people, and has been called upon to become a symbol of devotion and self-sacrifice.[11] There is something ecological about her expected death: she is part of the process of a dying culture.

The myth however does not acquiesce in the circumstances and validity of her being sacrificed, and is working towards an ethic which opposes martyrdom, an exercise of will which seeks to counteract the destruction of human life within the ruthless processes of 'mother nature'.

Civilisation: re-organising the primitive

How is it that no one in Andromeda's own community offered to slay the monster, but all were ready to offer her as a victim, a scapegoat? We begin to see some complex family and group dynamic in the background, something that goes with tribal life, particularly when social patterns are changing and the more primitive family existence is threatened by outside forces. Perseus, in a sense, comes in as 'family therapist', taking an outsider's view, and a morally purposive view: the perspective of a man whose boundaries are much clearer, by dint of the separations and confrontations he and his mother have made, than those of members of a close-knit family. Here the geography of the situation is important. Perseus's wings take him willy-nilly to Egypt and Palestine: King Cepheus is of Ethiopian origin. The Greek here is going back to something more primitive, to earth-goddess territory, 'old brain' land, and social organisation in which the ego and individuality is less defined than it becomes in western development. It is what we have come to call the Third World, underdeveloped, and open to exploitation. Cassiopeia's behaviour reminds one of the vain extravagances of the present rulers of some small African states and of their wives, corrupted by western habits of opulence. Andromeda is the beauty of African primitive culture, of closeness to nature, wildlife, body-life, which is in danger of being sacrificed in the cause of 'development'. The transitions which threaten the more primitive organisation (Cassiopeia must have felt threatened if she needed to boast) also threaten the organisation of the ego.[12] Andromeda's sacrifice is a sacrifice of ego leading to a reorganisation of ego: her loneliness and enforced separation from the family, symbolised by her exposure chained to a rock, mean a loss of her sense of self as part of an extended family ego: she either dies as a member of that dying community, or lives apart from it.

This crisis is faced by women as patriarchal societies begin to decay. Whenever a patriarchal tribe, a community or culture refuses (like Acrisius) to accept that its identity is radically changing, and denies the impending death, the feminine, the young woman, suffers most acutely from this denial, for she looks forward and outward and knows instinctively that she must 'marry out' as part of a wider networking process, or healthy cultural miscegenation: yet she is inherently and intuitively concerned with connectedness and continuation, racial and physical bondedness, and can feel chained by that: only the masculine ally can help her break the chains.

Andromeda is the third-generation woman in this process: like Danae she has a father who is absent when most needed, who fails to protect her and help her in the outside world. Cepheus was too weak to counteract his wife's inflated power. However, unlike Danae, she does have a mother who is present, and she is not imprisoned and enclosed: she is personally stronger and openly available: this makes possible her salvation and her more active contribution to cultural progress.

One young woman in a workshop who came from an immigrant Indian family felt Andromeda's situation acutely: she had suffered severely in her attempts to free herself into the British way of life and marry an English youth. He had had to use all Perseus's bravery and resourcefulness to deal with the belligerence and the attacks of the male bullies and female witches of her family. The family experienced British urban life as a corrupt monster threatening to swallow them and ruin their culture. Instead of trying to better understand and relate to British culture, they sent their daughter into that world naked, unequipped to deal with its challenges, but chained to their immobility. Since they refused to see her predicament and her despair (for they could not acknowledge their own) and refused to accept his love for her and negotiate with him, she had to be 'rescued' by him without the myth's subsequent resolution: they married without her parents' acquiescence or blessing and she cut herself off from them in great distress. Working through the myth in the workshop helped her to see how she was part of an inevitable and healthy process, and could trust that process.

Andromeda and Perseus have enough acceptance from her parents to validate their marriage, which is held on their ground: so they are given a positive ritual send-off. But they cannot stay in this environment. Perseus will head back to Greece as soon as he can, aware now that that is the home background in which he must make a new home. Greece means Athena, principles of wisdom and justice, civil organisation, city states, boundaried and protected islands, the safety of masculine forms and disciplines. But the myth is clear that before he can come into his own in that civilisation he has had to go back to Africa, right brain, old brain, Third World, for primitive, root strength.[13] He is now half of a partnership, a marriage of man and woman which is also a marriage of old and new civilisations, of Yang and Yin, of homeopathy and surgery, of time-bound purposeful definitive creativity and timeless processes of creative continuity serving a larger purpose than mortals can be aware of.

He still has to make a home in which he may become a father, find his own territory. Before he can do that he must confront and deal with the patriarchs Polydectes and Acrisius who have never given him territory in which to grow and have sought to kill him. He and Andromeda now have everything to live for, and need a base for their future together.

The individual journey:
laying the foundations for new ways of being

All that we have seen of the Perseus-Andromeda marriage is relevant to individual development. It is that stage of re-grounding after a transition in which one has freed oneself of some system of control or some outworn structure. Now one must establish a new order of existence and begin to integrate and synthesise experiences of the past and initiate new energy and new organisation. I shall look at this in greater detail in the chapters on creative process and body process; it is the place where new language and new form are made, new modes and systems of being are instituted, and a re-alignment process begun in the organisation of the body and its life, be it through body therapies or through changes in lifestyle. The re-formation of the relationship between body, mind and spirit is what is happening: at this stage all is tentative and exploratory; the art of learning is of the essence, as elements of the old self and the new are fused and ways found to express and move with the psyche's directions. People move house, change jobs, relationships, experiment, gradually re-organise their personality. This often involves going back to their roots, re-assessing their ancestry, discovering that 'home is where we start from' and realising that they have found a core self that was 'there all the time'. They begin to live in the present, on the ground of the here and now, more in touch with their body rhythms, instead of feeling tied to the past and rushed into the future. For those who have made deep transformatory changes through psychotherapy this is where the re-integrative process begins in earnest and modes are learned for continuing that process with or without help.

The new self has been born: it must now learn to live in the world; the 'true self' has been recovered, the 'false self' discarded. People dream frequently of babies, or of themselves as small children relating to adults: these are aspects of themselves getting into new relationship. And they have erotic dreams, of sexual mating, which reflect the inner re-alignment of masculine and feminine, the coming together of Perseus and Andromeda. As the 'true self' emerges they become more open and direct in their approach to others (much as is suggested by Lawrence's poem quoted above), cease playing games: their interactions with one another are creative, not repetitive of fixed patterns. Truth, and trust, are keynote issues, as they are in the Perseus and Andromeda story. But they learn too that the naked truth of Andromeda, its innocence and spiritual beauty, needs protection by the shrewd confrontative aggressive Perseus if the true self is to survive in a dangerous world.

Once this process has been initiated and the new modes of formation, movement and learning have been embarked on, they have sufficient strength to confront and discard the old forms and control mechanisms, to assess how these controls have kept a hold on them and how to relinquish that hold. That is the next stage of Perseus's journey: the killing of Polydectes and of his grandfather.

Chapter 9

Death of the patriarchs:
Endings and beginnings

Perseus does not look back – but he does go back, to the beginning – by way of Seriphos to Argos. He retraces his steps, much as one does in a psychotherapeutic journey, returning to look at the old scenes of one's life history in a new light. His first concern is with his mother and Polydectes: he goes back to the place in which he grew up but could not come to manhood: something must be resolved there. His second concern is with his origins, the place, the mystery of his birth. The myth doesn't clarify the extent of Perseus's knowledge of his relationship to Acrisius. It is unlikely that he knows of the oracle's prediction. There is a feeling, created by the silence of the myth, of some unknown guilty secret being tracked down. Was it maintained in silence by Danae? Perhaps Perseus has doubts about his patrimony, cannot believe his mother's story about Zeus – or whatever she has told him – suspects incest, rape, illegitimacy? There may be dynastic implications for him; but bound up with that is his sense of self as a man, his still elusive identity. And that depends on the family myth. We can never know what the 'truth' of our psychological history is: it is the story we are told, or that we tell ourselves, that 'tells', matters. Perseus goes back to Argos to find the 'truth' of his male identity, of his fathering, and it eludes him. Acrisius, the container of the truth, attempts to hide, absents himself, moves away to other territory. And there, on neutral ground, the secret truth of the past manifests in the actual event of the present: Perseus's killing of his grandfather.

In retracing his steps in search of his identity Perseus is accompanied by Andromeda: she who has known territory, home,

identity, but has gone on to suffer the loss of it and survive. Thus she becomes a supportive companion in his quest. This is increasingly becoming a role for women who have been through painful loss of identity; they are able to accompany men on a similar journey. Andromeda is true to her name. Mary Daly, the feminist theologian who believes all women experience non-being under patriarchy, puts this very clearly:

> . . . becoming who we really are requires existential courage to confront the experience of nothingness. All human beings are threatened by non-being . . . I am suggesting that at this point in history women are in a unique sense called to be the bearers of existential courage in society . . . People attempt to overcome the threat of non-being by denying the self . . . The only alternative is self-actualization in spite of the ever-present nothingness. (Daly 1973)

This last sentence describes exactly what Perseus's task is. Andromeda will 'encourage' him, give him heart, and doubtless comfort him, for he will find something of the self he is seeking only to lose it again: Argos is nothingness.

In returning to his 'fatherland' for the source of his maleness Perseus is also seeking kinship, ancestry, the blood-connection that is so powerful a tie and source of loyalty – and so often betrayed. Adopted and illegitimate children as they grow to adulthood go to inordinate lengths to discover and re-connect with the missing father or the original parents. Like them, Perseus is granted the knowledge and the connection for a brief time only, and must then bear the loss. Both he and Andromeda will be mourning that separation from the roots that is the lot of all who live through times of social reorganisation.

The return to Seriphos: temple and palace

Perseus first goes to Seriphos to resolve his 'unfinished business' with the father-figure who released him into adulthood and sought to kill him: the father of his adolescence, who so inadequately handled the growing boy's needs. This is where Perseus confronts the control of his sexuality: achieved firstly by keeping him trapped in the triangle the parents needed, then by jettisoning him into a world of Medusa corruption that was designed to paralyse and castrate him: a characteristic picture of what a decaying patriarchy does to male sexuality and creative power. Perseus effects an important and healing change in the scenario. He has, on arrival at Seriphos, no idea what has become of his mother. He had been told that Polydectes was going to marry another woman, a lie designed to mislead him. In fact Polydectes has continued to pressurise and threaten Danae and she, fearing his violence, has taken shelter, with the fisherman Dictys, in a temple. There Perseus finds them, and immediately goes to Polydectes's palace and kills him and his followers by holding up the Medusa head. He then puts Dictys on the throne of Seriphos, and takes his mother away with him to Argos.

The image of Danae and Dictys in the temple is a powerfully symbolic one, and for Perseus personally a needed reassurance: a strengthening of his feelings of security and rightness. These he needs before the killing of Polydectes, an act both of revenge on a would-be murderer, and of protection of other innocents, a destruction of what has become a cynical and untrustworthy regime. Danae has found the 'good father' and is reunited with him in a sanctuary, a place of spiritual devotion. There is a metaphor of reconciliation here, an echo of all the temples in which statues of male and female deities are found as consorts, marking the union of god and goddess. For Danae herself something is being healed; spiritual partnership, the finding of soul-mates, becomes increasingly important in later life, and time spent in retreat, in some sanctuary, with a kindred spirit, gives nourishment and meaning as the body grows increasingly weary of relentless, perhaps pointless, activity. As the sexual drives lose their dominance, Platonic friendships are increasingly valued. For Danae, self-respect is restored in such a place: 'When I go on a meditation retreat' said one woman, 'and keep peace with myself and with the men there, who are like brothers to me, then I know all the battles I seem to have waged against men, not to let them abuse me, have been justified.'

For Perseus to see that 'togetherness', his mother in communion with a soul-mate, gives added meaning to the killing of the 'bad father', and lifts much of the burden she has been, clearing the remorse he must have felt as an adolescent needing to separate from her. He is too again in touch with the first good man he ever knew, who saved him at birth: a father-figure who has spiritual qualities: the father in the temple. This is an important connection for him, and a memory of the previous landing on Seriphos: his emergence, as a baby; into the light, arrival on to safe ground, in the presence of Danae and Dictys.

So the accession of Dictys to the throne of Seriphos is, personally, a significant symbol, as well as politically a hopeful suggestion of a potentially benign leadership. Perseus, by effecting this change, gives himself a father-figure he did not have before, and a model of a good king. Such a symbolic act nourishes the psyche, and it is worth looking at the implications of this for the role of a monarchy in small democratic states like Britain. Without any real power, a Royal Family becomes a potent symbol.[1]

The return to Argos: the elusive father

Danae and Perseus, now accompanied by Andromeda, go back to Argos, back to where the story originated, and with this begins the attempt to recover and face the lost father, originator, ruler, controlling principle. For Perseus it is all a mystery, unknown territory, but territory he might by right inherit, a grandfather he might reclaim. But that is not to be. And for Danae to return to the home from which she was banished, the father who rejected her, there can only be a painful mixture of anger, fear, nostalgia, grief. How can she confront this man who ruined her life and prevented her from relating successfully to other men? She has come with her son, challenging Acrisius with the sight of this living Perseus whom she has brought up in defiance of all efforts to kill him. The confrontation does not happen: Acrisius runs away in guilt and dread from the woman and the young man who now to him represent inevitable death. Not only was it fated: they now surely want revenge for his treatment of them. With this evasion and departure he loses all moral authority.

A woman of 48 felt this very cogently, describing the recent death of her father. As a small child she'd been his favourite, but during her adolescence he'd turned into a relentless bully from whose tyranny she'd fled into a disastrous marriage that lasted only eight years, leaving her with two children and crippling financial burdens.

99

'He was ill for a long time and turned into a pathetic old creature. He expected me to visit him in the Old People's Home and be nice to him. I did do a bit, but I hated him, and his sourness . . . He treated the nurses dreadfully. I wished him dead, and he knew it. I couldn't pity him: I felt he deserved to suffer after the way he'd made my mother and me suffer. But somehow I couldn't say to him, to his face, "Look what you did to me. It's your fault my life's like this." He slithered out of it – just like Acrisius – he knew it well enough – so he retreated into being senile and pathetic and sorry for himself. He never asked how *I* was, wouldn't listen if *I* complained. After a bit I stopped going. Yes, it did kill him – he died soon after. And he didn't die well.'

Subsequently the same woman, aware that she was still seeking the absent father, needing love and support but not letting men into her life, had the following dream:

'I was in my house, and cleaning myself up with neatly folded toilet paper, having just relieved myself. But on the floor there were a lot of little children and babies: they might have been dead, or just quiet, I don't know – they certainly were to do with the mess I'd been cleaning up. Then my ex-husband was outside the door wanting to come in and I said he could: he had the key – which isn't in fact true. And my father came in too, but my father young as I knew and admired him when I was a little girl.'

So the process of recovering the lost fathers involved letting them see the mess they had made of her life, and her good and bad products. She was cleaning up the mess single-handed in her therapy, giving up her own feelings of shame and guilt, and allowing herself to confront the ex-husband and the memory of the young father who had abandoned her. It is Perseus who does the final 'cleaning up' in the myth: he has the masculine capacity to deal with the Polydectes and Acrisius to whom Danae is still subject, and to restore 'left-brain' order and meaning. The woman dreamer saw that she herself could use her own masculine Perseus: she related the neatly folded toilet paper in her dream to her own work as a seamstress and presser with a couturier – a craft she pursued with a devotion taught to her by her young father who was a tailor's apprentice before he became a middle-grade civil servant and a very frustrated man.

100

For Perseus, the disappearance of Acrisius, his abandoning of authority and responsibility, his refusal to meet his grandson, must also produce a feeling of shame and humiliation: this way Acrisius still has a hold on him in Argos, still denies his identity and existence. The resolution has to come elsewhere if Perseus is to take up his own authority.[2]

The 'cleaning up of the past' is enacted in the Larissa funeral rites, where the dead body or the ashes are buried, like faeces, in the earth to which we must return. Perseus, in killing off the super-ego control figure, has to experience his own loss of control (of the discus), before he can take charge of his life and of his own products, has to make meaning of death. All this – the 'tail end' of the story – is part of the resolution of the basic anal conflicts that lie 'behind' much of our philosophy of life. These are usually dealt with at the end of a personal therapy: we have to go right back and undo the initial control system and organise a different way of taking charge of our own process. (This may involve 'killing' the therapist also, if the therapist's system has been too controlling. Many women have had to do that to their male Freudian analysts.) And one therapist maintains that when the client allows himself to fart in the therapist's presence, the process has come to a satisfactory ending. I shall look at the effect of anal complexes on the ego-formation process in chapters 11 and 12, but it is worth mentioning here that one of the greatest revolutionaries and challengers of the fathers, Martin Luther, who effected *the* Reformation, was obsessed with anal fantasies and sicknesses which constellated his struggles with the devil and his war with his own father. This is all documented in Erik Erikson's *Young Man Luther* (Erikson 1958).

Funeral games at Larissa

The funeral rites are essential boundary-markers, acknowledging ending and affirming continuity. Acrisius, in attending them, must face the fact of death he has so long tried to avoid. Perseus finally makes the fatal patrilineal connection, in the setting where a dead king is being honoured, where simultaneously there is 'vertical' time-measured activity, connecting with the ancestors, and 'horizontal' space-measured activity, competing with the peers: father–

son links and brotherhood links. This is a safe context for the death of Acrisius at Perseus's hands.

In one improvised modern version this scene was set in an American political party convention: the patriarchs of the corrupt old order were being replaced by the younger generation, of whom Perseus was a leading challenger, finding his strength through political competition. A particular feature was the strong 'thieves' honour' and sense of loyalty and peer allegiance between the 'guilty patriarchs', as they saw themselves forced to bow out. This impressed Perseus, who felt unexpected respect for them even as he had inevitably to oust them. His onslaught brought Acrisius to death by heart-attack: at the point of dying the old man recognised his banished daughter's features in the youngster's face.

This version highlighted the issue of authority inherent in any hierarchical regime, for whatever one may feel about a fallible patriarchal ruler – or father – he has been put in that position by the collective, and has been obliged to fill it, to take the responsibility few others would wish to take, and to take the blame and the condemnation. He is trapped by the situation. Acrisius, given the limited choices available to him in his fear, could hardly perhaps have been other than he was. Ultimately he has to be forgiven and his humanity acknowledged.

The mystery and quality of male power needs to be better understood and respected. (It is too easy to throw out the baby with the bathwater of patriarchy.) The rituals that go with it are of particular significance, for they reflect and constellate masculine connectedness. Women have their body-orientated, intuitive connections: men need structures, symbols, language, the matching of strengths in the outer arena. The oral folk music tradition has a feminine quality; men have been masters of the finest music for wider performance. Competition in the service of raising standards is a masculine quality.

Male tradition and continuity manifests through the handing on of craft, knowledge, wisdom, through many generations: sadly much of that has been lost and the handing on of property and propriety has increasingly taken its place. This has led too to the discrediting of male discipline and cultural ritual. The son of a German ex-soldier felt his father's 'absence' for him was due to his denial and negation of his past under the Nazi regime which he could not talk about to his son. He prevented him joining anything faintly militaristic, even the boy scouts, and the youngster therefore received no initiation into masculine 'mysteries'. He now feels he must re-assert the masculine through effectiveness in organisation, at the same time incorporating the feminine in that work. 'I am re-presenting my father' he says, 'and must do it on different ground. I can't keep fighting the patriarchy – I have to go *sideways*, start afresh in conjunction with the feminine.' He has come to the same resolution as Perseus.

The need for the father: the 'pattern', 'patron', the guiding principle is strong in men, and ritual helps them meet that need. Again, in the context of mourning, a young man whose father had left the family when he was ten reported the following:

> 'I went away on a church weekend and talked to one of the
> pastors about my relationship with my dad and how it affected
> me. He told me to write down all the things I felt about my dad
> and the things I wished I could say to him, and then put the piece
> of paper in the collection box and by so doing 'give' those
> feelings to God. I remember it was quite upsetting to do it. The
> last two lines of what I wrote said "I could never love him . . . I
> could never touch him". I cried after writing that.'

The male connectedness here is striking: God, priest, absent father, son; and the therapeutic quality of the mourning ritual is clear.

For men to resolve the issues they have with the weak and guilty fathers and grandfathers may involve subtle political or complex theoretical work, for the masculine influence has predominated in all areas of thought, conceptualising and control. The confrontation with the patriarch is basically, however, about the use and abuse of power, about betrayal (see Hillman 1964), the last words on the Cross, very often betrayal of the feminine aspects of experience, the tenderness or forbearance that might have existed between father and son, denied by the 'tenderness taboo' (Suttie 1935) and the fear of homosexuality. British male writers are increasingly dealing with these issues and it is often in the context of cultural change, the impact of education, the outgrowing and rejection of a working-class background.[3] Betrayal seems mutual between father and son: but in writing the novel, the poem, the play, the sons are honouring the fathers – and carrying on their fathers' traditions as craftsmen. Making a formal ending is part of self-formation: arts and crafts contribute vitally to the capacity to do so. Not for nothing was the mortal father of Jesus a carpenter.

A recent cogent example of patriarchal revaluation is John le Carré's novel *The Perfect Spy*, where the quality of fatherhood and manhood in the male chauvinist world, as experienced by three generations, is ruthlessly exposed. Though the confrontation with the weak treacherous father is made at a personal level, the implications for the world of political power are clear: the whole international network of relationships is a dangerous sham façade based on shabby ideologies: trust is a dead concept. The central character of the novel, who has reviewed his late father's legacy of impotence and betrayal, now himself on the verge of suicide, of absenting himself, tells his son that in writing this confession for him and ending his own life, he becomes the only possible bridge of transition between grandfather and son, hopefully enabling the son to live an uncorrupted life. The meaning of generation is poignantly clear here and the novel has finally a ceremonial quality as the father goes through the rituals that will make his own funeral.

Honouring the 'guilty patriarch' is in itself a compassionate recognition of human fallibility. Hareton's reaction to Heathcliff's death in *Wuthering Heights* is a deep wholehearted grieving and respect for the man who had dispossessed and degraded him – but had many years back saved his life by an involuntary regretted act of protection.

The remorse felt by Perseus, the guilt we feel when we know that our actions or thoughts have 'killed' an aged parent, helped a dying tyrant on his way, is a necessary accompaniment to an inevitable process. In it we acknowledge our difference and ensure we do not copy the sins of the fathers, at the same time recognising that this destined death was inevitable and our responsibility for it minimal. Identification with Perseus at the moment of killing his grandfather is a dramatic one, for the elements of the involuntary are so powerful in suggesting destiny and spiritual meaning: he is half aware of the mysterious energy, the train of events that has brought him to this place and moment:

'I feel this wonderful power and strength throwing this discus: it feels great to be competing with other skilled and strong men, with my wife and mother watching me too. And then to see the wind catch it: I'm horrified seeing it kill him – and then to discover who he is – terrible, like a devastating warning to me about my strength, and chance, and fate, and climatic events we don't understand . . . I feel I don't ever want to throw a discus again. Like when you drive a car and have an accident and don't ever want to drive again – but you have to, of course.'

The man who said this then added:

'It's like space satellites and weapons, and how they are thrown out with such pride of achievement, competition, but accident – "human error" – can make them lethal. We have to learn our limitations . . .'

Coming up against the limitations, discovering the boundary by transgressing it, accepting death; Perseus must experience these in order to define boundaries in the process of ego-formation, of self-development. This is well known to analysts of the psyche (see Gordon 1978). In terms of body energy it is succinctly expressed by Stanley Keleman: 'My awareness is actually the process of my excitement thrusting toward form. The unbounded finding boundaries is what awareness is' (Keleman 1975b). This seems an excellent way of describing Perseus's experience in throwing the discus, and is borne out by the words of the man quoted above.

The meeting of Perseus and Acrisius, the 'formal' setting, with its impersonality, is facilitative: ritual promotes drama, has the detachment of art. The drama is played out that makes meaning of the co-existence of life and death: the story is rounded off and ended in the presence of onlookers. It becomes a ceremony in which Perseus is initiated into mature manhood, and the oracle is fulfilled.

The masculine rites of the Larissa games, associated with male athletic 'mysteries', depend on qualities which need restoration in our world. The loss of discipline, the laxity that has blurred boundaries and blunted moral refinement have robbed us of the power to make meaning. James Hillman puts it thus:

When the father is absent, we fall more readily into the arms of the mother. And indeed the father is missing: God is dead. We cannot go backwards by propping up senex religion. The missing father is not your or my personal father. He is the absent father of our culture, the viable senex who provides not daily bread but spirit through meaning and order. The missing father is the dead God who offered a focus for spiritual things. Without this focus,

105

we turn to dreams and oracles, rather than to prayer, code, tradition and ritual . . .

Perseus is soon to become a father himself, and is learning here about focusing the spiritual, about moral order.

The mother encourages her son: go ahead, embrace it all. For her all equals everything. The father's instruction, on the contrary, is: all equals nothing – unless the all be precisely discriminated. (Hillman 1973)

Hillman is offering a corrective to the blurring, merging, intemperate tendency of the feminine, the loss of precision which can occur when the male influence is absent. He speaks from an American perspective: the British version can be seen in those who have grown up in a 'liberal', 'progressive', perhaps 'pacifist' family, where there has been so little discipline, containment, definition between the members of the family that the ego is feeble, the self-assertion that of a spoiled child. Aggression and destructiveness are frowned on, their essential importance as boundary-setters unrecognised, and everybody is 'nice': the children beat their heads against mother's feather-bed. When the accumulated vital anger erupts in one or other member of the family it is uncontained and shockingly violent.

It is important for Perseus, the destroyer, whose right arm has been used to murder in the service of the feminine, to learn now the limits and hazards of the power of that right arm, as he does at these games. His aggressiveness and combativeness can be channelled into competitive sport, yet even the boundaries that provides may be transgressed by misfortune. But they must be kept. The lesson for us could not be more timely, for the practice of sport, and the conduct of combative wars, have now lost all sense of boundaries, safeguards; they have become areas of indiscriminate destructiveness and violence.[4] The struggle to maintain the Olympic spirit is marred by the parallel absence of spirit, humanity, respect, in political and military conflicts. This is another example of 'symbolic equation': the game, or the war, has ceased to be an 'area of play', of matching strengths or resolving differences, and has taken hold as a psychotic reality. Don't confront, restrain or negotiate with your foe: annihilate him. It will be part of Perseus's maturing (as it must be of our whole civilisation's) to continue to

106

discriminate, for he has been close to the mentality of the annihilator in causing the deaths of Polydectes and his court and of Andromeda's suitors. The slaying of the Medusa, the killing of Acrisius, are of a different kind, and between them all he must ponder on which of them has a meaning which gives him honour and does not degrade him in his humanity, and which have allowed an indulgence of his destructiveness.

The *I Ching*, one of the greatest sources of patriarchal wisdom available to us, comes to a conclusion that is similar. The final hexagram 'BEFORE COMPLETION',

> . . . indicates a time when the transition from disorder to order is not yet completed . . .

> > The image of the condition before transition.
> > Thus the superior man is careful
> > In the differentiation of things
> > So that each finds its place.

> One must separate things in order to unite them. One must put them into their places as carefully as one handles fire and water, so that they do not combat one another.

'The transition from disorder to order is not yet completed.' It will be up to Perseus and Andromeda to make order in a new setting, to compose rituals and structures which will accommodate new needs and make new meanings.

Beginnings

After the closure, the end of Acrisius's story, Perseus, out of grief and respect, and doubtless judging it inappropriate (interesting word), will not take Acrisius's throne in Argos: he moves to other territory and sets up his own dynasty. This is a healthy 'shame' and enables him to start afresh in his own way, on his own terms, free of Acrisius's legacy of repression and of mother-in-law Danae's possible interference or undermining of Andromeda, since Argos was her domain. In this decisive shifting to new ground to make a new home, Perseus shows himself again as the one who, having killed the Medusa, can whenever need be break with the past. He establishes his own authority, and authorship.

We now see how Perseus, at this point of death, of separation from Acrisius and Danae, re-enacts his own birth as we commonly do at such major points of transition. As suggested in chapter 3, he must have fought his way out of a constricted and constricting womb, a terrified and terrifying mother. Whatever destruction was required would leave him with a feeling of shame, remorse, at his own seemingly excessive aggression, which was inevitable. The same happens in the killing of Acrisius, who originally caused that womb to be a prison – Perseus is too strong for him. This is another birth, and the decision not to go back to Argos, which would be going back to prison, a womb, in terms of an emotional or political regime, is part of it. Shame becomes unhealthy and turns to guilt if we do not recognise that the birth, the destruction of the parent, is vital to the creation of new life. Acrisius denied that truth and tightened against the life and death process: inevitably therefore he has to be violated by the new being coming to birth.

After some consideration in a workshop of Acrisius's story, we pondered on how it might have been different had he reacted otherwise to the oracle. One elderly man, himself already a grandfather, said,

> 'I would have heard it, with sadness, as a statement of the inevitable. I would have thought about its meaning for me and my grandson, and made sure as he grew up that we both understood and accepted it, so that he need not feel guilty and I need not feel afraid of him. And I could even see myself, say, having a dreadful disease as I got older and asking him to have the strength to kill me, to give me something to end my life . . .'

What, then, of Perseus's father Zeus? Is it he, Danae's inspiration, who gave her the breath of life, who now sends the wind, the breath, that deflects the discus, reminding the humans of their helplessness before climatic unpredictability, the will and the destructive power of the gods? Perseus is in touch here with his spiritual fathering, bringing to him the experience of humility and compassion needed by a spiritual leader, giving him truly the strength which destroys tyrants, the right arm an instrument of a finer power, rather than a dealer of retribution.

Students of the Eastern martial arts will see here a correlation with their practice and philosophy, and appreciate that Perseus at this stage is fairly well, but only temporarily, grounded in his relationship with Andromeda, and on Larissa territory. He has yet to feel fully grounded, well planted on his own two feet, to achieve maturity in his way of being. Then his aim will be better focused.

Mindful of the god his father, Perseus cannot consent to a return to Argos. Taking Acrisius's throne would mean ruling over people who have become habituated to his way of exercising power: too much energy would have to go in the struggle with them. 'Alternative' movements are fully aware of this, knowing that they must be free to build their strength through experiment and experience, away from the traditional regime. The strengths of the old tradition can be better assessed when viewed from a distance; the context must be changed: Perseus learned that from Pegasus.

Compromise is not possible between a truly new system and a dying system. Collaboration, some overlap perhaps, but there must be separation. This enhances respect and tolerance, which only wisdom can provide: humility and compassion – and a sense of humour. It is lamentable that the dying patriarchal system is so rarely confronted and openly, constructively, challenged. Without such clarity everyone's credibility is compromised. Political leaders become buffoons or nonentities, treated without respect, never taken seriously, fast becoming TV actors in dramas nobody is responsible for directing. They behave accordingly, increasingly alienated from those they purport to represent, and from consideration of principles, and they fight for their existence on stage instead of retiring gracefully.

By contrast, the 'retirement' of Danae from the story, her silence in the background, is particularly significant. She is present, silent, and vital to continuity, and her non-interference is a matriarchal virtue. Her voiceless role is explored further in chapter 12, but here it is clear that watching the drama unfold is important for the healing and integration of all she has endured, and for the development of wisdom.

A widow of 50, whose only son had recently married, spoke of the paradoxes she now experienced:

> 'I feel both young, newborn, and yet old: I know I'm ageing. But the new, fresh learning about how my body's changing feels young . . . I look at my son's marriage and see Perseus and Andromeda, and though I have some envy of their youthfulness and energy, that I'll never have back, on balance it gives me great

pleasure to see their togetherness. And I want to be both of them, and can be: a bold adventurer, risk-taker, like Perseus, but taking care of the vulnerable young Andromeda in me too: my body . . . Of course there are times when jealousy and depression and greed start to threaten me – the monster. But I know now that it can be dealt with – I've survived that before. I've got the Medusa's head in my pouch!'

Reminding her that the head then went to Athena, a goddess of wisdom, helped her to see how she was becoming a wise woman – a role too little acknowledged and therefore not as yet very much built on.[5] But it will need to be, for the wise older women must take over where the foolish older men fail. And they were there first.[6]

For the myth began, of course, with the wise age-old oracle, with feminine wisdom. The Delphic oracle, the omphalos or navel, and other oracles were surely the voices of the earth-goddess, and the patriarchs turned to them when they needed their wisdom. Until asked for their opinion they were silent. It is characteristic of their status that only after I'd worked with this myth for several years did it occur to me to suggest in a group that we identify with the oracle. Then each person, seated on the ground, was able to feel the profound, sure power within them, and the necessity for silence – and for riddle: this was based on compassion, as they watched the affairs of human beings take their course. There was no question, at the end, of 'I told you so', only of an added, sad affirmation, and increase, of that wisdom they had. One older woman said 'I feel as if I'm coming into my own at last . . . if I can be recognised for what I know and have learned in my life, I'm happy to retire and let the young get on with their life the way they have to.'

The future lies with the younger generation, but are they being robbed of it? Disenchantment and cynicism so easily disempower them, as does the degrading condition of unemployment. They need help to shift ground, as Perseus and Andromeda do, in order to reclaim their creativity, to find a system which is not dominated by the depression, personal and economic, which is their parents', a space in which they are not paralysed by the spectre of the Bomb and apocalyptic visions, but can begin to cultivate trust and hope.

The myth applies to each one of us personally: we have inside us different 'generations': creative projects and potential developing anew out of old experience. Casting off the ineffectual over-controlling masculine and the depressed feminine which we have internalised, which have threatened to dominate us, is vital if we are to start afresh with a newly balanced bisexual energy as the basis of our living, our work, and our loving.

The new dynasty

I leave it to each reader to imagine what the new dynasty is like – an exercise which will be for you the gift of this myth, its offering to the creative imagination.

Whatever regime you visualise, it fathers and mothers Gorgophone – the free feminine spirit who refuses to die in the holocaust demanded by the patriarchs and goes on to find another masculine spirit that is still alive. By detaching herself from the dictated fate of death on the funeral pyre, Gorgophone marks a new stage of enlightenment and civilisation, a refusal to accept as inevitable the fulfilment of the universal male death-wish, the big orgasmic bang.

She has come to that as a result of generational experience: her grandmother and her mother, as well as her father, have had much to tell her. Danae, Medusa, Andromeda before her all experienced being sacrificed by both male and female malignity. The achieved relationship of her parents, the banishment of victimhood and martyrdom from their way of living, give her a basis of self-worth and self-respect which make it impossible for her to throw herself away. (A fascinating parallel, in the context of our times, can be seen in the book by Kim Chernin, *In My Mother's House*, describing four generations of women. It is visible, too, in D. H. Lawrence's Brangwyn women.)

What Danae has watched, the resolution, and the equality in the marriage of Perseus and Andromeda, Gorgophone inherits as a birthright. Her name, which may mean 'killer of the Gorgon', reminds her constantly that her father destroyed the most victimised and corrupted of women, and therefore the most dangerous. We need reminding: we easily forget that, like Perseus, we each have it in our power to recognise and then deal with the corruption and evil that accumulate within us; and opt for, then work for, the good. His example makes him the guide we need, the father who has been too long absent.

Chapter 10

Absence and presence
Conditions of fatherhood

To some extent it is father's business to be absent: away hunting, earning a living, functioning in the wider world. In many cultures it has never been expected that he would stay with the family (Green 1976). He is able to be free therefore of the body-ties that the mother experiences as the nurturer and dweller in the nest they build. He can, too, be detached from material concerns, the everyday: he can absent himself, in a spiritual, philosophical sense, from the mundane. This accords with the masculine logos function: pure contemplation, rationality, idealism. And it relates to the 'schizoid' state: to practices of meditation, mysticism, contact with the eternal, with the spirit of the ancestors. 'Abstraction' is a better term to use here than absence. At the same time the father can bring these principles down into definitive form or ritual, into the family, and help to clarify the boundaries to material, fleshly relating. In everyday living father prevents mother and child from overmuch merging, insists on the cord being cut. From his perspective he can see that it must be, and so he healthily serves the life-process.

However, father's absence has become pathological. If he brings nothing back to the family that has any meaning for them other than the material, his necessary detachment has failed in its purpose, is in fact not detachment at all. The mundane life of the flesh, of dependency on the material, begins to dominate in the family: a perversion of maternal nurturing ensues, and the suffering experienced forces a flight from the family's pain. It is usually given to father to act out this flight (unless an older child has already done so for him). He is, by role, and by virtue of the male tendency

113

towards schizoid withdrawal, the obvious candidate. At one and the same time he is being scapegoated, and resented because he has seemingly got off scot-free from the crisis. He easily takes on the role of the 'irresponsible' one. But the irresponsibility is the whole family's, and the wider social context is irresponsible also.

Acrisius is one such father. Unable to achieve the philosophical detachment the oracle requires of him, he adopts physical and emotional detachment, fleeing from pain, becoming irresponsible. In his place appears Zeus, divine father, sky god, pure spirit who comes to mortals in story but is otherwise unreachable: abstracted, absent. He has limited power on earth, the territory of fertility goddesses, but he can negotiate with them. The complicating factor for the western psyche now derives from patriarchal monotheism: God is absent, elevated and controlling from a distance: the one and only, up in heaven, with a representative on earth: Christ, or, for Jews the Shekhinah, the feminine presence on earth – a weak and scarcely acknowledged deity. Everything was created once, and really fundamental creativity is not expected to happen any more: the earth goddess lies dormant. Or so He says. This model lies behind many men in relation to their families. We need bitheism and polytheism to restore their spiritual creativity. The increasing influence of Jungian psychology, which cultivates the restoration of feminine–masculine balance and explores polytheistic myths to find meaning, suggests that is already happening to meet our religious needs. (Freud, who was unable to solve his monotheism complex, offered little at this level of need. In many ways he is the Acrisius and Jung the Zeus for the Danae of psychology and psychotherapy – I leave readers to play with the rest of the story.)

Our loss of the extended family – which was reflected in the family of gods on Olympus – aggravates the situation, for the nuclear family puts too much onus on the parents to be god-like, to carry all the responsibility that could be shared with a wider community of kin: the burden can easily become unbearable. And the burden on a father who is expected to play God is one he, hardly surprisingly, may be happy to give up. He will feel impotent and be blamed for his impotence – but his wife and children need to acknowledge that it is the whole family's impotence that is projected on to him: the whole family must find its collaborative creative power (perhaps with the help of family therapy) – starting probably with the impotent mother, whose frustrated and perverted

114

creativity is projected on to and avenged against her husband. Theologically, there must be a re-assessment and revival of goddess-figures if God's fathering is to improve.

We are back to absent mothering. Acrisius has no visible or effective wife, Danae no mother. She has been effaced, is perhaps dead, or banished because she will bear no sons. Mother's absence is a deeper initial threat to our existence than father's: so is her presence, if she smothers or castrates us, in the birth or later. Acrisius's hard-heartedness could have been tempered by her balancing intervention: perhaps his coldness was a withdrawal from the pain of his unsatisfactory relationship with her.

Absence experienced: the need for mourning

We experience the absence of others in many ways; we 'miss' them in head, heart and body. The deepest and most threatening experience is of abandonment, loneliness and isolation: it calls up in us the baby who might die, whose spirit often does die, when it is starved of physical contact, heartwarming, nourishment, mental stimulation: its world becomes filled with fear, anger, grief, and unmanageable fantasised monsters of hatred. Adults' needs for love and attachment are no less – if they lack ego-strength they will succumb, regress to the infantile state and go crazy – as many do in enforced solitary confinement. Danae surely would not have survived her sea-chest journey sane were it not for the presence and needs of her baby.

In a wider sense, the personality, or the family, like the body within its skin, needs containment, holding, definition. Father, the masculine, tends to provide that. But if the containment, holding, definition has been too restrictive and controlling, its sudden withdrawal seems catastrophic. Closeness and distance are crucial conditions. The 'gaze of men' indicated by Barthes (quoted above, page 5) may be an important container for women, resented or not.

The feared extremity of abandonment described here lurks behind all experiences of absence and loss. As a result much of the separation may be denied, or blurred by unsatisfactory periodic visiting, or avoided by 'filling the gap' with other people or activities. But the unresolved feelings about an absent husband-father always resurface in other relationships, or are turned inward to the detriment of the family's health, physical or emotional. The absence compounds the problem: it's not possible for a family to vent its feelings on someone who isn't there to receive them. In marital breakdown, the legal divorce procedure often marks the first formal ritual of death of the relationship, and usually arouses a welter of emotions that have been concealed, in some cases for years: the pain is severe, but it must come out and be experienced. It is a question of bereavement and mourning. The pain of absence must be accepted, the intense feelings that go with loss and abandonment must be expressed, and time must be allowed for whatever healing is possible, with or without professional help.

This is vital, and I stress it because it is the one important aspect of the life process that is missing from this myth: there is no *explicit* mourning, weeping or comfort in the story. We are free to imagine the fears and tears, the mutual comforting, the remorse; but they are not shown. There are funeral games: mourning is instituted, but we are not told how it happens, and somehow the 'lubricating' effect of weeping on the mechanics of the story is missing, and it might be possible to enact it with a dry stiff-upper-lip heroism. The watery element, the energy of Poseidon and the Nereids, is a threat: floods of tears might rock the boat, devastate us. We must not get wet.

What is missing is the feminine quality that facilitates mourning: the mother who helps daughter and father to separate, who comforts those who are bereft, the wife who helps a man face mortality, the earth-mother who sits patiently with those who are in pain, takes their rage and sadness, and facilitates healing. There isn't an earth-goddess in the story, only the sky-goddess, Athena, who is too busy doing, being active and mindful and judgmental to sit quietly and receive our sorrows. The representative of the fertility goddess who can convert the compost of life, who accepts the cycle of destruction and creation without moralising, transforming our blood and shit for new growth, the healer Medusa, has been relegated to a cave and paralysed. It is significant that her eyes, and ours, are the media for that death-like state – they do not weep: we do not melt, but turn to stone. The severely depressed Medusa condition is usually reinforced by the inability to cry the needed tears of frustration and deep sadness.

Gorgophone's action is also significant: it is not simply heroic defiance; we must recognise that she is rejecting a patriarchal rite that denies the opportunity to mourn, separate, go on to new life. She will be able to experience her bereavement.

The denial of loss, the male taboo on weeping, the incapacity to share pain and give comfort are disagreeable features of patriarchy, often designed to deny the loss of the feminine aspects of life, as well as to deny the fact of death. Boys are supposed to be tough, not tender, mustn't miss their mothers, must grow up to be hawks, not doves. Only *in extremis*, such as in army life in the trenches or in Japanese prisoner-of-war camps, do men allow themselves a fuller humanity, since old-style heroism is meaningless in such circumstances; corruption and death cannot be denied. But in male-dominated politics, commerce, technology, it is all competitiveness, success, power, toughness and controlled corruption. Failure, loss, despair are swept under the carpet as far as possible: gloating, not sympathy, is likely.

This aspect of patriarchy has been adopted unwittingly by many self-liberating women, who refuse to acknowledge that in extricating themselves from their dependency on and submission to men, they are losing the love and support and allegiance of men. The worst imbalances of feminism arise from that denial. Those divorced mothers, or lesbians, or separatist feminists, who pretend they can do very well without the absent man, refusing to mourn, fail to make a proper separation, and are always dependent and tied to the male and to his ways, and dominated by his absence. They too take the heroic stance – and it sits ill with the ugly hostility, blaming and bitter recrimination that often surfaces in their contact with men: Medusa characteristics.

Proper separation is fundamental to the capacity in each of us to be present, to live in the present reality. As long as we are still with the absent one, unconsciously or consciously, we are not wholly alive and present. We cannot live in the 'here and now' if we are still holding on to persons and events that are somewhere beyond our reach, or exist only in the past or future: we become chronically absent ourselves.

One young woman, daughter of German refugees, feels her parents are never present, but always in Germany, in the earlier homes and the death camps with their lost, loved ones. They never mourned properly, never let the past go, and are absent for their children here in Britain. 'My parents never look at me, always through me', she says. She herself has the same lost, sad but unweeping look in her eyes, difficulty in focusing on people, constantly yearning for the closely felt mother's presence that has eluded her since birth, and constantly smiling in a pretence of denying the family's´ continuing, unresolved distress. Her brother meanwhile acts out in grossly anti-social behaviour the violent feelings that lie behind the dry-eyed family smile.

The Absent Father's experience

Fathers vary in the degree to which they can tolerate the disparity between the role they thought they were to adopt and what fathering has turned out to be. If they began fathering with some degree of flexibility of attitude and this was shared by their wives, then the whole family can create a role that is not fixed but grows and changes. This will accommodate separateness and absence, even in the extreme situation where divorce and the setting up of another home occurs. This flexibility is perforce coming about as more and more family breakdowns occur, and the new generation of fathers and mothers obviously have to take into account now the likelihood of this happening.

The challenge at present is to get the absent father to return: whatever that means in its context. What seems to have happened is that the fathers who have been banished, or have withdrawn themselves, are still in a state of shock, not quite sure what has hit them, trying to avoid feeling the pain, guilt, bewilderment, and vaguely hoping the mothers will sort it out for them. The mothers do their best (by writing books on the subject, for instance) but that isn't enough. The absent father needs to contact his inner Perseus, work through the feelings he probably has about his wife, family, society and the Medusa proportions they may have assumed, and go on to use his imagination and all available resources to help restore his sense of himself and his potential as a man and a progenitor. No woman can do that for him: she can lead, like Andromeda, but her view is limited by her biology, and if she insists that her imagination can provide answers for him then such omnipotence inevitably takes away his responsibility.

Very few 'absent fathers' attended the Absent Father workshops:

those who did were, on the whole, emotionally confused and needing to stave off the impact of the women present, who were confident they knew and could express their own feelings. That the workshops were run by two women is also noteworthy. It is not by chance that we found ourselves unable to trust any 'absent father' enough to co-lead such a workshop with him. In preparing this book, I contacted five divorced men of my acquaintance (five whom I know to be more than averagely self-aware) and asked for their comments on how they had experienced their separation from their families. One responded immediately (I quote from his letter below); two were incoherent to the extent of offering nothing; two did not reply. So they keep their absence, and I can only make them present in this book by registering that. And I was led to wonder how far the absent father's womb envy leads him to damage the mother's nurturance of her offspring.

Those 'absent fathers' who have come to psychotherapy for help have felt pushed out, isolated, abused by wives and by the law, guilty, angry and as a result acutely uncomfortable and vulnerable when relating to their children. To get comfort for their pain and sense of failure is not easy: friends will oblige with dinner invitations and introductions to other women, but won't talk about the distress of the separation: as ever, the evasion of bereavement, and a blurred condition of absence and presence. Ultimately the absent father can only really return if he has really gone away. Few have done that clearly enough to be able to make constructive meaning of their absence.

When he is ready to see the positive nature of what has happened, and take responsibility for his action in leaving the family, the father can look at the four 'absent' fathers of the myth and evaluate them, validate aspects of them that might have been rejected, by common consent, but need attention. Acrusuys, to his credit, did not kill Danae and Perseus outright. Zeus's qualities are of inspired insemination, the healthy non-attachment that frees Danae from her prison, and trusts her to mother a needed child, the implicit challenging of attitudes to sex and the meaning of life. There is the goodwill of the fisherman Dictys who was poor in material goods but not in spirit, and remained quietly available in the background; and the generosity of Polydectes which continued until he was too sorely tried. The mortal fathers here, trapped in the system, have positive qualities to be valued. But it is Zeus, the

119

immortal father of Perseus, who most needs exploring by the father who has lost his way and lost his role.

For the father who contemplates a return of any kind, another myth may offer something here: Odysseus's return to his home and the 20-year-old son Telemachus whom he has never seen (see Graves 1955). Penelope, the feminine, has kept faith: Odysseus, radically changed in personality by his adventures, arrives unrecognised and disguised: he has to reclaim his place with help from his family.

This tells us something about the conditions for return, and we can apply it to actual family situations, or to the return of the father principle, the reclaiming of fatherhood itself. What seems important for women to recognise is that Penelope's weaving, marking the passing of time, making artistic form out of her experience and her loneliness, weaving a tale perhaps, is not completed, can't of its nature be completed, because that would be to let in the usurpers, those who were never exiled, and would exclude and annul the experience of Odysseus, which is a vital gift that can be handed from father to son.

The condition of exile is an important one to look at: he who has gone into exile, in whatever way, for whatever reason, is in a special relationship to home, may perhaps never feel 'at home' again anywhere, becomes a nomad. But what he learns in his wanderings is a flexibility of role, an ability to be different, a new philosophy of life. For the absent father this must mean a new concept of paternal power, in which attachment and non-attachment are valued in ways other than they have previously been.

The two pieces of writing which follow I include for the honesty with which they express the experience of absence and disconnection. The first, in poem form, is by a man who did not want a child (he was estranged from the expectant mother) and relinquished all rights to his son soon after his birth. The second is by a father of four children, now all grown up. Both have that essential quality of emotional exile which acknowledges loss and therefore leaves the way open for revaluation, re-creation.

In some religious thought, the redemption is expected to come through the deities who are exiled and awaiting return (Perera 1986), who share their alienated condition with humankind and promote reconciliation; Jesus, the Shekhinah, and other goddess figures. Danae, exiled from Argos, belongs with them also. When

absence locates for the father a femininity that exile helps him to
reclaim, there is hope for the future.

Success

I have given away my son,
And all the years of patience and of love
And inexperience is what I've gained,
To appear virginal when I am grave,
And travel lightly, having cut the root.

I envy the honest gardener
Whose burdened back and aching heart
Tell of the passion that has nurtured him,
Caring for small lives in a green garden.

His roots are deep, his human eye
Beneath the gravid brow blossoms with joy.
And he grows more ancient and more youthful
Who has been sound, and sweet, and simple.

And the sophisticate with painted face
Ruined beneath its acceptable grimace
Squeezes life crudely, squanders the juice,
Tramples the discarded carcase.

I could take on that comparison
Out of self-hatred, for retribution.
The truth is, I gave away my son
Being young myself, having ambition
To enter a harder race. I was not wise,
And harnessed neither burden nor remorse.
I stumble from success on to reverse,
And even if I win, you are my loss.[1]

So what I would say is that I was really always an absent father,
from first to last. In any real emotional or personal sense, I was
not there for my children. Even the one bit of good fathering I
remember, when my youngest son walked out of school at the
age of 10, and I welcomed him at home and was very supportive
of his decision, he doesn't remember. So it is a sad sorry tale to
tell, and I very much regret the way I behaved, and wish I had
learned sooner about being a human being.

I am sure in the years to come they will be going to their therapists and railing at me and my absence, and they will be quite right. The fact that it was the best I could do at the time doesn't alter the fact that for them it must have been awful.

When I meet them now, the hugs I get are less warm than the hugs I get from total strangers. There is a stiffness in our relationship which I don't like but can't think what to do about. I see my grandson from time to time – I think I get on better with him than I did at the same age with any of my own children. I have learnt something, but it's all too late. How sad.

Sad it is, but I question that it is 'all too late.' Something was learnt, but perhaps there is more to learn . . . that it's never too late. While I was working on this book, and preparing to write the chapter on the death of the patriarchs, my own father died. It confirmed my belief that this myth had come to me when it was needed, preparing the way for the patriarch to die and giving me the task of making meaning of that death. His Acrisius-like treatment of me many years back had drawn me to Danae's story. The myth was tapping into, reflecting movements in the collective: my family, the many people I work with, and wider society. At a conference on violence and spirituality I attended shortly beforehand, a weekend much concerned with the decay of patriarchy, I dreamed he was dying. When it happened ten days later I realised how much the Perseus in me had been driven to somehow willing and bringing that about, to avenge my inner damaged Danae. My first reaction was certainly not one of love and forgiveness, such as I'd found possible at times in the past, but inordinate rage, and joy in the release of life and love in those around him he'd suppressed, though he still seemed to rule from the grave.

I'd intended to write about 'honouring the guilty patriarchs' but hadn't the heart for it for some time. Then I realised how ritual, the 'funeral games', formal mourning, was important, for it would enable me to pay the respect due to any human being who passes over the boundary of mortality and to ease my remorse: Perseus's remorse. Since we are Jewish, there was some mourning ritual, but it was partial and inadequate, almost meaningless, for the religion had no hold in the family: he had been unthinking, ambivalent, as a guide. And since, like Acrisius, he had no son, the extended year-long mourning, the daily saying of the Kaddish prayer for the dead parent, did not happen. Patriarchal Judaism does not expect a woman to perform this rite: a few have nevertheless done so. I could choose to, but I seem to be adopting another way of paying respect to his life, in the context of the absence of a religious connection with him, which is in the completion of this book: a different kind of ritual.

It has made me realise how the absent father, by his very absence, fathers creative work in others.

Section II

Myth and process

Chapter 11

The myth and creative process

It has long been recognised that most major creative works are in themselves statements about creativity and models of creative process.[1] The myth of Danae and Perseus, with its central concerns of death, sexuality, and birth, offers a unique body–mind–spirit pattern of that process. Working powerfully on the psyche and relating closely to body experience, it mediates at the boundary between mind and body in that search for spiritual meaning which is implicit in all creative work.

The basic mode of forward movement in the myth, as in most creative process, is that of *holding and letting go* (control and surrender) and of *symbol-formation* (at the point of letting go), a process in which the personality, and carnate experience, are progressively, throughout an individual life, finding and making impersonal and transpersonal meaning. This symbol-formation is Perseus's creative activity.

There are blocks to creativity, and negativities which have to be dealt with, because pain and fear demand it: but there is always available another basic positive mode of creativity (that of Pegasus) which is in itself transpersonal – or collaborative – and not always conscious. It relates to the 'hidden order of art', a kind of organisation of collective wisdom which the psyche taps into, finding itself a transmitter of spontaneous creative manifestations. Gregory Bateson's view of mind as something universal, not individual, tallies with this (Bateson 1973). It is the area of dreams and of the free poetic: the imagination, seeking form, surrenders to it and acts within and 'around' it. This making of art in relation to the collective is a kind of ecological imperative: it is there in the garment woven by a tribal woman, and in the Bach oratorio. It is celebratory, ritualistic, and space-oriented (because it knows its own place in time), whereas the individual struggle to find identity and emerge from confinement is time-oriented. This individual mode predominates in the myth until the death of Medusa – thereafter Pegasus introduces an expanding creativity.[2]

Both modes are healing. The therapeutic process and the creative process are very similar, and there are different modes of psychotherapy which correspond to these two ways of healing.[3]

The myth has already spoken for itself in the preceding chapters: my observations here will focus more directly on its patterning of creative and of therapeutic process. This corresponds directly to body process, which for greater clarity I look at separately in the next chapter – but they are inextricably linked.

The chief sources of my theoretical understanding of creative process are literary critical theory and the work on the psychology of creativity deriving from the schools of Klein and of Jung.[4] One book has proved invaluable in bringing these influences together: Rosemary Gordon's *Dying and Creating*, and I have found it remarkable how closely the Perseus myth tallies with her findings, in particular the four stages in ego-development she discerns in the creative process (Gordon 1978). Gestalt therapy has made significant contributions,[5] and these offer a bridge to body process, linking with Reichian and bio-energetic understanding of the creative energy of the body, which in its turn has considerable resemblance to Eastern understanding of body energy-flow (Keleman 1975b). Recent work on the birth process[6] has shown how it becomes a matrix for life development: this initial experience of individual creation is reflected in all subsequent creative endeavour; in individuals and in wider social groupings. Moves toward the 'redemption of the feminine' have inevitably proved how vital that is to creative progress, and the work of James Hillman and of feminist therapists and theorists such as Marion Woodman has been very influential. Literary and linguistic developments and trends in music over the last twenty years have paralleled this. Dance, drama and psychodrama and groupwork have been powerful media for the development of collaborative creativity, as has film-making.

128

Acrisius: form and decay

Acrisius is everyman who wonders why he is not producing the offspring which will be a visible mark of his productive potency. Dissatisfied, feeling inadequate, he takes to the oracle the question we often pose ourselves 'Why haven't I produced something worthwhile?' (Marion Milner's classic book on creative process is entitled *On Not Being Able to Paint*.) The oracle in its wisdom (a wisdom we have in ourselves but may deny or refuse to listen to) tells him that his limited understanding of creativity is in itself a reason for decay and sterility: he must bow to the inevitability of its decay. Acrisius is form, structure, theory which has become too self-centred, rigid and controlling, determined to define and direct in its own way, unable to conceive, reproduce anew, nor allow that it is only part of a generational process. The more ego-investment (kingship) there is in the form and its power, the more it will fear its own death and resist the impulse to creativity, freedom, new birth, of Danae. Here is the initial refusal to let go, the holding on to power. It can happen in indivdual or in collective creativity. The structure tightens and locks up its own vital energy but, as a result, makes the pain, the tension of sterility so acute that the unacknow-ledged divine spark, the creative impulse perforce must come in to inspire and inseminate new birth. Danae, feminine-passive to Acrisius's masculine-active, is helpless, but nevertheless the vehicle of inevitable creative continuity (the Receptive, in I Ching understanding). However much the old form seems to have a hold on us, we trust that if we wait, receptive and passive, letting go to the process, the new will begin to come to birth, though we may have little awareness of its nature, and no way of conceptualising it within the old restrictive framework or language. There is the hint of an idea perhaps, a glimpse of possible new form, or maybe only a dim sense that something is lying dormant that is soon going to come to life.

If the tyranny of the super-ego's censorship is absolute, the impulse to freedom is bound to come from rebellion. Though the rebelliousness is at present confined, it is there and will emerge and overcome the control. That too we know, half-consciously, for our inner oracle has told us so. Sometimes we deliberately close and tighten, Acrisius-like, in order to evoke Danae, Zeus and Perseus.

This, of course, is characteristic cellular behaviour: putting Danae in a cell unconsciously invites reproduction. People often put themselves under acute stress in order to reach the point where they have to seek therapy.

Zeus: 'divine inspiration'

What implants the 'germ of an idea'? Every creative artist knows that it does not originate in our own conscious thinking: it comes as a gift, seemingly out of nowhere, manifesting in a sudden flash of insight, or in a dream, or in a number of associations which suddenly gel and grasp our attention. Free fantasy, free association, play, activities which tap right-brain resources may call it up – or 'down', since for more sophisticated creators there is a sense that a state of readiness, together with a confidence in process and their willingness to create new form, brings in the god who wishes to speak through them. Also, Danae's feeling 'I've got to get out of here', her need to be free of the imprisoning form or structure, leads her to call on whatever is outside that structure, more powerful in its larger view of creative purpose than the limited and mortal form which holds her. A client may have a similar fantasy about the therapist, and most therapists do provide the vital initial inspiration to those ready to receive it.

Here we have the essential paradox of creativity: is Zeus within us or outside us? He is an inner fantasy of an outer force: a human imagining of the non-human which gives meaning and perspective to humanity. He comes as a symbolic shower of golden rain: and we find ourselves asking whether he then turns into a male body, carnate and sexual, or impregnates Danae in a non-human, semi-natural, semi-symbolic way. In himself he lives in the realm of make-believe, at the boundary between fantasy and reality, death and life, where most creative work goes on and bridging symbols are made: Pegasus's area. He comes to Danae to impregnate her with renewed capacity to symbolise. The son she bears, Perseus, is himself a 'border-line' person, half-human, half-god. The 'border-line', near-psychotic state, in which fantasy and reality are precariously interfused, is experienced, more or less distressfully, by many creative artists. The inability to symbolise, to mediate between fantasy and reality, can lead to psychosis. The artist, like

Danae or Andromeda, may reach a state of crazy hysterical frustration, fear of annihilation of self, unless and until the symbolising work can occur. Perseus is the symbolising force: he will give meaning to Danae's existential crisis.

The intense frustration caused by sexual need is similar to, and sometimes produces, the intense pressure felt at times by creative artists before the sudden inspiration comes. It seems then that the creativity can manifest either with or without genital sexual activity, sometimes sparked off by it, at other times becoming a channel for the displaced energy. This should not be dismissed in a reductive cynical way as 'sublimation'. It is love that we need to give and receive: the pain of being prevented in the body leads to self-love and thence to other ways of creative loving. Masturbation, auto-eroticism, is closely associated with this and often precedes or accompanies the excitement of creativity in artists working in isolation.[7]

Thus one can inseminate oneself with one's own inner Zeus – a dream, sudden revelation, or sexual fantasy. Or one can receive the physical or psychic insemination from another, who is then a symbol for Zeus. One's position is definitely receptive, feminine: a dream can't be forced to come. And the need is for procreation. The sexual meeting, real or metaphorical, is in the service of the creative impulse: an occasion for 'baby-making'. Women and men both tend thereafter to discard the partner emotionally in their dedication to the project.

Zeus, who frees us from our prison, may come in any guise, and not always recognised: golden being or opportunist, satisfying or peremptory, violating and despised or comforting and welcome. The impulse to create can be experienced in any of these ways when it takes hold of us. And our experience of the human father Acrisius, his forms and concepts and language, will inevitably affect our concept of the imagined father Zeus. Danae is freed by Zeus to give life to Perseus, but she herself will always have an attachment to the old form in which she was reared because Acrisius never granted her her freedom. Perseus will have to deal with that later: he cannot survive with her limited view of what father is. He has a different father, and must discover what that fathering means.

Perseus: birth of a full-term idea

An idea 'whose time has come', an articulated concept, a work whose ultimate completion is now a declared intention: this is Perseus born. What was a notion developing unseen within is now 'out there', visible to its creator and to others. It is now a responsibility, a commitment. Since it embodies a drive towards freedom and new life, beyond the old constriction, it needs nurturing and protection, particularly in the initial stages. New projects are vulnerable to attack by all who are threatened by their growth: Acrisius will do his best to impede Perseus's progress by abandoning him and Danae and banishing them from his support system. For creative artists this may be the ostracism by society, by critics, or, in their own inner process, the sense that the outworn form offers nothing at all to the new concept, has let them down when they most needed the safety of an appropriate structure. They are adrift now, speaking a different, still tentative and very young language, nothing like the firmly established one they had so long used and depended on – and at this stage translation or compromise carries the risk of betrayal.

The two things that keep us going through this phase, when the survival of our project and of ourselves as creators seems so precarious, are the conviction of the 'divinity' of this brainchild, a sense that we have been entrusted with a gift, and the memory of its coming to birth. The pain and difficulty with which ideas struggle to emerge in the face of opposition and misunderstanding, and often in a context of fear and loneliness, add to our sense that they are particularly meaningful, since in themselves they carry a fundamental truth about survival and freedom, about death and rebirth. Even if this is in a purely local individual context of one small-scale creative project, or in one person's fight to change stifling life circumstances, we know that it is a symbol for, and part of, a much wider human urge toward freedom and wholeness.

The birth itself, the struggle out of the imprisoned and imprisoning womb, becomes a matrix for the creative drive, with the artist both mother and baby, Danae and Perseus. Our attitude to childbirth, to pain and suffering, to the conditions of our own coming into existence, influence this, setting up tensions of holding and letting go in this existential crisis. Survival for what? Why

132

bother? – is a question that often challenges a motivation which comes mainly from within.

The crisis of an unsupported bringing to birth will be recalled in all the subsequent life-transitions which punctuate the process of individuals or people. Wherever the containing system has rigidified some freedom-seeking seed will be implanted in its womb, and creative people will go, unsupported, through a struggle which is more or less painful, violent, to be born through and out of it: in that struggle they face death, confront fundamental threats to their raison d'être. For the individual, a therapist may be chosen as a womb for a new personality which needs to be born, and will become Danae to the client's Perseus.

Such half-awareness of significant destiny is Danae's in the lonely directionless obscurity of the sea-chest. Her devotion, the 'primary maternal pre-occupation', and the post-natal depression, are both features of the process. The artist cherishes and clings to the work, very identified with it, at once exaggerating and doubting its value: others don't help, can't understand. This enclosure by the feminine, womb-like in itself, protective, unguided, relying only on inner trust, isolated, may be suffocating. At the same time the artist may feel 'all at sea'. In the process of the therapy, the problem roughly identified, therapist and client have committed themselves to set off on their journey together, and may feel both cosy and daunted by the task, though they need to float freely at this stage. Clarity, a sense of direction, a supportive structure or energy will soon have to be found, lest the project die for want of air and light.

Seriphos: new ground for growth

A new form, language or structure is found or adopted to accommodate the artist and her project. Dictys brings them into the open air and finds them a refuge. This may be a more amenable patronage in the world outside, or an adoption of a more flexible form, a system which allows the ideas which were unacceptable elsewhere to be expressed and explored. A person who has hitherto been stifled by an orthodox religion or political party or a suffocating marriage may convert to a new religion or party or marriage. In this new form the work grows and flourishes as it could not in Argos.

Yet, in time, Polydectes turns out to be too much like Acrisius. His generosity and patronage are conditional: he wants to appropriate and control the feminine. The new structure begins to feel as uncomfortably rigid as the old, and the project gets stuck in the old form-versus-content conflict, and doesn't know that it needs to transcend this conflict. The depressed feminine is struggling again with the over-controlling masculine, and the essential sexuality, free creativity, is locked up once more. For the individual artist or writer this is a bewildering impasse, a place where some innocent trust in what one is doing seems betrayed. What has gone wrong?

Writ large, it can be seen in dramatic clarity in history. The freeing of the Russian people's spirit by the Zeus of Marx from the Argos of Tsarism, took them to the Seriphos that later became Stalinism. The background of severe deprivation, the desperate need for survival, aggravated the situation. The tensions of holding and letting go, passionate feeling struggling against strict form, are manifest in the great Russian literary and musical works of the nineteenth and twentieth century. Erik Erikson relates this condition, interestingly, to the Russian custom of tightly swaddling babies in infancy (Erikson 1965).

In Europe, nineteenth-century culture evinced the attempt to express the new feminine 'romantic' spirit in an old masculine 'classical' language. It took the meeting with the Medusa of the First World War and the break-up of form that followed to allow the creative feminine to express itself more radically in the work of Eliot, Picasso, Schoenberg and others.

In the realm of the psyche itself, psychology, Freud initially played a Zeus role but had too much of the controlling patriarch in his make-up: his 'permissiveness' rigidified and kept the sexual-creative feminine from truly expressing itself.[8]

Holding and letting go: again these are the issues in the relationship of conservatism to innovation. In individual creative work, there may be a tendency to hold on, in a comfortable rut perhaps, over-identified with the work, enjoying an immature Perseus position of defiance without real change. Or, like a nervous Danae, the creator protects and idealises the work, which in effect limits its potential, ignoring inner and outer hints that things have got stuck. Pride, and fear of further abandonment, prevents her from letting it go. In therapy, the therapist becomes blind to the impasse that may have developed in the interaction.

Perseus breaks free

Ultimately boredom or irritation with the stagnation set in. There is then a sudden change. The client thinks of giving up or the therapist's supervisor gets exasperated. The impatient stepfather structure refuses to accommodate this tedious project, and jettisons it. With this drastic letting go, the project takes on a life of its own. Suddenly characters in a projected play or novel start to speak for themselves, and act in unpremeditated ways. A poem or musical work begins to re-write or run away with itself, taking its bewildered creator into unforeseen regions. Freethinkers break with the adopted religion or political belief or second marriage and begin to express themselves honestly and recklessly. It is a time of exhilaration, and uncertainty: the shock of the new. Perseus is suddenly realising his own strength, and doesn't know what to do with it. The Polydectes in us has an easy answer to this awkward burgeoning of free creativity that doesn't fit the pattern: kill it. If it thinks it's so clever, send it off to face the real harsh world: that'll soon put a stop to its idealistic nonsense and it won't survive. The artist can be quite cynical about the value of this new departure: he will not give it an easy ride, and may adopt a safe shallowness.

Into the Medusa's cave

The project is being put to the test, and is now at a critical stage. Perseus, an adventurer with independence and pessimism thrust at him, is expected to be a hero: he is not equipped for this. The client in therapy shifts into the previously concealed 'negative trans-ference': suddenly the therapist looks malign. Going into the Gorgons' cave is a life-and-death time for the project which now must work through its essential identity crisis. The creator's relation to the work is interrupted – the old tie and apparently benign control mechanism is lost – and what was a comfortable nurturing Danae quality in the author changes to a Medusa that threatens to kill off the new spirit altogether. (This can be seen dramatised in the Wilfred Owen poem quoted in chapter 1, written at the point when benign Edwardian patronage suddenly turned into parental slaughter of the innocents.)

The artist is stalled, blocked. The threat stops many in their tracks. Projects are abandoned, temporarily or permanently. Danae and Polydectes withdraw: their conflict has ceased to be the basis of the work. Perseus meanwhile gathers strength and support to confront and slay the Medusa the two have created between them: which is, the assumption that the project cannot now survive. The artist is up against it: that negativity which is most powerful when the creativity is most fundamental. It is where the questionings begin, undermining our conscious safety, touching the unconscious and plumbing the realms of death and non-existence, that we find the blocks to our creativity, and the perversions and corruptions of it that threaten us with stasis, sterility, or madness. Perseus, however, has resources, some imagination, and faith. And he knows himself to be half immortal. True creativity never dies, though the creator in his old form might.

Medusa: envy and creativity

The complexity of the Medusa has been explored in chapters 5 and 6: she is, on first meeting, all negative things to all men: a corruption of the feminine by the masculine. In the creative process she may be within: a powerful holding negativity, a constipation that paralyses, or she may be without: an institution or person that does the same – and the two reflecting one another will of course perpetuate the stasis. The institution may be a political regime, or the publishing or art-marketing world, a mute conspiracy of envious critics, the media, a 'mother church' set up by the fathers to stifle creative spirituality, or the institution of motherhood itself: a Virgin Mary or Jewish Mother, each a corrupt version of the goddess. The institution or envious personality seems to overpower us completely, for it subtly encourages self-hatred.

The Medusa within is a compound of envy, resentment, refusal to budge, unexpressed rage, humiliating self-criticism, and a cynicism or trivialising blandness that negates every creative endeavour, one's own and other people's.[9] At its worst one feels caught, fixed in obsessive introversion, blind, dull, worthless. The Medusa closes around the offspring that cannot be born, becoming increasingly toxic. And she is mentally constipated, stubborn, not wanting her offspring to be born: she envies it the way Acrisius envied Danae's child. All this negativity plagues the head, for it was mental Athena, born from Zeus's head, who cursed her.

In the presence of the Medusa intense depression sets in, and paranoia as the artist begins to feel persecuted by the project itself and the demands associated with it. Where the Medusa outside has become too powerful, as in totalitarian regimes, the creative artist or dissident will in fact be persecuted, annihilated, or led to commit real or professional suicide. In less drastic situations the equivalent fate threatens or haunts the creator, who goes through a crisis of relationship to the work and to those for whom the work is done, a crisis in which the true meaning of the work is both lost and found. Perseus sees in the mirror that there is far more – and less – to the Medusa than she, or others, believe: that she is not lethal, but transforming at the deepest level: not an annihilating negativity but a challenging one. Life and healing is in her and comes through her – but through her body and blood, not her brain. Those who recognise in their work and its impact the creative potential of the dark goddess and can cut away the mask-like head which falsifies her will survive, taking with them the new strengths and under-standing of process that she brings. Wilfred Owen's poetry, unafraid to incorporate the vileness and sickness of war, did just that.

The underworld cave is a place of transformation, and the serpents on the Medusa's head are a reminder of the shedding of skins. The spirit of the work (and of its creator) is uncomfortable in its old skin, form or body and must change that form: despair and suicide – real or metaphorical – are close because of the inability to visualise the new form. This can apply to small works of art and to the political creators of our world, threatened by suicide.

The feminine knows about process: her stuckness is about products – the anal-patriarchal insistence on producing something admirable in a defined time. For these products the Medusa has no imagination, which terrifies the composing, discerning masculine quality in us which needs completion and enlightenment, cannot bear to be unproductive and in the dark, fears chaos and cessation. The threat of dark nothingness has itself to be looked at. It is resolved – in time – and seen by Perseus to be an illusion, for he is a new source of illumination, an image maker. His task in the Medusa's cave is to 'realise', with his mirror, her symbolic and therefore transient status – not fall prey to symbolic equation and take her for a fixed reality. It is in a similar underworld, in his poem 'Strange Meeting', that Wilfred Owen meets the mirror enemy who is the friend. It took the horror of the Medusa war to re-establish that human image.

People involved in a creative project which goes through a depression must find the meaning of the depression itself. The same can be said of economic depression. The project has been based on a misconception or outworn concept which is now stuck; the ego, over-inflated, is suddenly aware of how hollow it is. The letting go of the concept seems like death. And the civilising father who makes meaningful forms is absent. In therapy, the client may feel close to annihilation or suicide, having lost her self-concept.

Perseus's resources

Misconception and misperception are related. Athena's mirror-shield provides the means, through reflection, through the image, to changing one's perception of the Medusa, altering the concept that she paralyses us, and cutting off the deadhead. Athena, fiercely virginal, whose virtue is in resisting seduction, promotes genuine confrontation, a straight yet sideways look at a Medusa who can easily seduce us into fascination with her negative power.

The sickle of Hermes is suggestive of the hermetic qualities that can be used in art and life to get round powerful obstacles: humour, satire, trickery, secret codes, allusive and elusive language, sideways manoeuvres that cut through the ponderous authority and heavy solemnity of seemingly immovable ideas. Satire in particular handles the negative or disgraced energies that other modes cannot accommodate: 'black' comedy, the writings of Swift, the work of grotesque cartoonists.

The shield and its use are an example of the 'transitional object' and 'transitional phenomenon' as defined by Winnicott (1971). For the infant, these media of play facilitate the transformation of relationship, the finding of identity and separating out child from mother, 'me' from 'not-me'. They are essentially symbolic, allowing definition beyond a condition of symbiosis. The symbolising involves 'the whole work of mourning'[10]: this implies the expression through art or therapy of the feelings aroused by the loss of the other, and the achievement of detachment.

This playing gives the time and space for creative endeavour: it is an 'area of permitted illusion' which is at the basis of all art, and of the psychotherapeutic alliance. Truth and fiction blend temporarily and then separate out. By contemplating the Medusa's image in the mirror, Perseus, detached and separate, assesses what this figure is to him and symbolically kills the negative holding power over him of Danae. The Medusa's status is firmly realised as symbolic, and Perseus's too-close relationship with Danae and the structures that have been binding him is dissolved. In therapy, the therapist will have become the Medusa for a while for the client, who can then examine what she has projected on to the other.

The capacity to make symbols is a uniquely human attribute. In the continuing search for meaningful selfhood the need to find symbols for one's existence is vital – especially when existence is painful, and death seems inevitable or preferable, as it may well do in the Gorgons' cave.

The symbolizing process via the transitional object normally comes, in Kleinian terms, alongside or after the schizoid-paranoid and depressive phases, and facilitates the emergence from the latter. Similar to this is the creator's relationship in these crises, to the environment, the potential audience of society, which is the 'Kleinian breast' that nourishes the dependent artist (Segal 1979).

Insofar as the creative process replicates the birth-process, the cave, like the encircling society, is the womb – an inimical toxic environment. At the end of the birth-canal looms the forbidding mother-cervix threatening a stop to movement, the end. Perseus has to realise that this is a place of birth, not death. It parallels the 'No Exit' phase in the birth process, when the baby feels interminably trapped, unable to move prior to the final forward struggle to emerge (Grof 1975).

This experience of existential crisis may come with such threatening intensity perhaps only once or twice in a person's life – most commonly in our society during and after the middle years. But to a lesser degree it is there with all major creative transitions, life stages, and in the metamorphosis process of major original works of art. It can be severe for those artists who are most sensitive to crisis in the collective. They 'play out' in their work the social sickness, as a means of finding health for themselves – and discover that they must detach from the collective sickness in order to survive – as does Perseus.[11] The isolation and dislocation experienced in this negative place is acutely painful. It can be eased somewhat by the understanding and support of others who recognise the frustrations and distress of this blocked condition, but know that it is usually a prelude to a breakthrough, into something startling in its originality. Meanwhile it is a dis-ease. In therapy it will be worked through, and sat through. One must trust that Pegasus will emerge when the work of Perseus has been done and the deadened energy shifted.

At some point one is ready to cut free and cast off what seemed to have an immovable hold on one: a particular form or influence, a relationship with a controlling or envious person, a powerful dogma or theory, a part of the work which was important initially but is now transcended and needs to be torn up, cut out or pruned (with Hermes's sickle), or one's own tedious negativity and pride, one's inner Medusa head, which is a 'pain in the neck' that needs to be let go. These are almost all 'heart' phenomena which puzzle the head, and one thing that does need to be seen in the mirror-shield is that there is power in the rest of the body: metaphorically, for the group or nation, and for the individual, literally. Simply at an everyday level it is easy for creative people to become so involved in head activity – big-headed even – perhaps in very sedentary positions, that they fail to draw on their body's vital energy, and their health, and that of the work, can become impaired by neglect.

In conceptual terms, the 'changing set', the shift to a new paradigm, the change of perspective, is never a conscious head-directed activity. It comes usually as a surprise, discovered, unthought-of.[12] Facilitation of this movement by the 'Focusing' process developed by Eugene Gendlin (1981) works through a 'felt sense' in the body, not the mind. And it can often happen dramatically through physical release of energy, change of breathing, and other Pegasus-type movement: a shift of viewpoint occurs which theorising couldn't achieve: the body releases the head from its obsessiveness.

As Stanley Keleman says: 'The body's resonating lights up its powers of cognition. The brain is the servant of the body, not vice versa' (Keleman 1975b).

Pegasus – transcendent imagination

The Medusa slain, Pegasus is born, and with this breakthrough the energy is suddenly quite different and the expansive imagination takes flight: an escape from the inbred morbidity into wholly other dimensions. This transition has been largely described in chapter 7: here I would point out that this is a sudden shift to the second of the two modes of creativity described at the beginning of this chapter. The creator has been caught in the individualistic drive which has much to do with ego, personality and boundaries: the struggle with negative immovable forces or forms to manifest one's separate self as the author of one's life. It has a left-brain, linear thrust in time. This now gives way to the freer creativity which is lateral, right-brain, feminine, floating in space, timeless, painless, formless, but also in touch with the collective unconscious and tending therefore towards collaborative, ecological, harmonising, poetic activity: transpersonal considerations, beyond the individual ego and its needs. Detachment, impersonality, are key conditions: 'non-orgiastic experiencing' (Winnicott) or 'art emotion' (T. S. Eliot) transcend emotional over-involvement with the work. Pegasus is unsentimental. The free-floating state with its separateness from the mundane is the distraction, the 'absent-mindedness' recognised as very important for creativity (Milner 1950). It is relevant to the issues of absence and presence explored in chapter 10. And it is a condition of greater contact, at a psychic level, with others: often the only means of contact. Poetry works at an unconscious level and the poet surrenders to that, knowing that the poem exists 'out there', beyond its creator's control: it is common property. Dreams have the same transpersonal status.

The two modes of creativity: those of Perseus and Pegasus, may exist separately at different times, but most fruitfully they come together: the greatest works of art are able to express the individual struggle within the transpersonal medium – such as Shakespeare's tragedies. In psychotherapy the eclectic practitioner seeks to combine the two modes, or uses them in the order suggested by the myth. (It is a veritable work of art to use them together since each requires a different role of the therapist.)

Approaching the essence of this fusion of the two modes, from the perspective of women's creativity, Lesley Saunders observes:

'One of the paradoxes of creative work is its dual role, celebratory and confrontational, its location at the heart of both stillness and struggle' (Saunders 1987).

Each time a work of art is completed there is the danger of egotistical satisfaction with it. Most accomplished artists are impelled by 'divine discontent' (the wings on Perseus's feet?) to go on, in the continuous process of formation, 'crystallisation', followed by recommencement: basic cellular process, the continuing search for meaning that is Perseus's life. If we look at Shakespeare's own process we see how each tragic hero transcends his own egotism too late – if at all. Each is unable to handle the feminine – the woman within or outside. The soliloquies manifest the painful tension between the personal struggle and the transpersonal poetic medium. The last plays – *The Tempest* and *The Winter's Tale* – go beyond the tragedy of egotism to a resolution in which the two kinds of creative expression merge to make something wholly new, in a form which, by the old standards, seems formless.

This is where the Perseus/Pegasus polarity shifts to the Perseus/Andromeda marriage, in which the two modes combine to create something wholly new: a third force. For Perseus can't mate with Pegasus . . . he can hardly harness him; no one can stay on his back for long. Since Pegasus is renewal, release – fresh inspiration, aspiration – he must be free and separate, not tied down, always available to take creators into unimagined dimensions and regions beyond the earthbound and the narrow self-centredness of set form. He is the principle of selflessness and therefore of love, in touch with infinity and eternity and the mysteries of cosmic harmony and of subtle rhythms that the human heart responds to.

The danger (real or feared) is that, after the initial thrill of soaring off with Pegasus ('falling in love'), he might run away with us, as our excitement leads to delusions of grandeur or romantic infatuation. It is possible for the artist or visionary to take flight from ordinary life, lose contact with reality, meandering in the realms of fantasy, indulging in the near-psychotic 'pandemonium of images'. It resembles an LSD trip, and can even become a similar cult. Such an escapist, potentially schizophrenic state is more likely if the previous negative holding has been intensely threatening.

This crucial stage, of transition and grounding, reflects the birth experience. If that was agonising and followed by traumatic isolation from mother the sudden loss of containment leads mind to split from body. Grounding, the healing reconnection with mother's body, restoring communication, is vital for sanity. Pegasus in fact suggests the needed balance: a horse, not a bird, he has four legs and potential groundedness. He does land, exchanging nourishing energy with the Muses, thereby suggesting that 'free love', fantasy, must find form. Even a state of wordlessness can find expression in music or art when a language is needed to communicate the as yet inarticulate. Pegasus can be temporarily tamed.

However, though Pegasus resembles the newborn infant in the pre-verbal state, still blissfully aware of 'intimations of immortality', he has not the human infant's problem of needing to find words, and of having to accept the reality that in the mortal world there are already many words, and they may not match his immortal awareness.

Perseus comes to earth

Perseus has to come down to earth. Though the right-brain knows about language and there is an organic hidden order of art, the actual words and forms and organisation must be found to convey to others the 'intimations of immortality'. That is the left-brain's business, and the more masculine ego takes over again for that purpose. Free imagination now gives way to 'active imagination', and there is further symbolising. Coleridge's similar distinction was between Fantasy and Imagination – the 'shaping spirit'. The masculine now knows its need for the feminine: not the threatening but the threatened feminine. Perseus meets Andromeda, to complement his personality, find and make love and beauty on earth, in the body, in form. She, significantly, is literally chained to the earth: to harsh reality.

The new forms begin to be constructed with care out of old and new formal experience, and the artist sees the possibilities of establishing a totally new relationship with audience and environment and with the projected work itself. Where there was conflict, frustration, there is now partnership and a sense of purpose. In the therapeutic process, client and therapist will be in a more equal, adult relationship as the client integrates the negative material and the threatening shadows that have surfaced from in-depth exploration. The 'false self' has been discarded with Medusa's head and the true self reborn: the strong sense of freedom, of love released with Pegasus gives new meaning to the therapeutic work. I have described this phase of development at the end of chapter 8. The creative arts are an invaluable medium at this point, and find their parallel in fantasy and dreamwork, Gestalt therapy techniques, the use of 'active imagination' in Jungian therapy, in psychosynthesis or in systems of spiritual practice taught by religions – usually within a non-authoritarian mystic tradition. Behavioural techniques and approaches such as Transactional Analysis also have their value here. The client will find many resources and media and learn how to trust her use of them and discriminate between them.

Before full commitment to the new task is possible – the marriage of Perseus and Andromeda – her plight, the vulnerability of the feminine, must be dealt with. The artist must know how to protect and preserve this in the face of the exploitative greed of Poseidon's monster. Access to the basic 'innocent wisdom' of Andromeda, with its earth qualities of tenderness and strength, involves the courage to confront squarely all that threatens the primitive faith and capacity for simplicity whose survival every creative person must ensure. Without it, the work is meaningless: there is a 'naked truth' that must be in dialogue with and nourish the creator's mind and mental purpose. Most artists have a concern for morality but a distaste for moralising: in the process of exploring life through art they can only negotiate with their inner faith in private commitment: to expose it to the outer context is dangerous. Yet, as Lesley Saunders says, in a sensitive examination of the paradoxes experienced by creative women: 'I don't want to lose sight of the commonplace that all art is made in a political environment.'

And it is easy to 'lose sight of the commonplace'. If the creator's purpose becomes, like Andromeda's environment, greed-orientated, easily seduced by the vain, egotistical attractions of fame or money rather than motivated by devotion to the art itself then the essential truths will be prostituted or sacrificed. In our cynical society it is easy to become cynical and greedy oneself, and ravage one's own innocence. The capacity for simplicity, like Andromeda, lives always on the edge of terror because in its sensitivity it is easily swayed, seduced, being a surrendering, receptive principle. The protective masculine has to give it stability and boundaries, and it must honour not victimise or rape this feminine tenderness.

Courage and encouragement are needed to preserve heartfelt truths: diligence also, to find a way of expressing the complexity and power of love, when the language is debased and every word for loving has become a mockery or a cliché.

Andromeda's exposure can drive her crazy. With the defences gone, the fear of losing the ground of one's being and one's own truth can pitch any sensitive person into hysteria or paranoia, and the loss of that ground into madness. The voice believes it is crying in a wilderness, and the art may, again, become psychotic, disintegrative, form for form's sake, or private fantasy essentially unavailable to others. Or it can become the she-monster, devouring everything mindlessly in its need for revenge: much pornography is that. A form must be found which contains or dissolves this potentially disintegrative quality of the feminine: the desperate hysterical vengeful goddess power misplaced. The marriage of Perseus and Andromeda is a commitment to finding that form.

Return to Seriphos and Argos – revaluation of old form

In the search for that form the creative worker, like the client in therapy, has to re-assess the relationship between form and content that was set up previously, the unhealthy relationship between the false and true self, or between the ordering masculine and the feeling feminine.

Learning, investigation, is the key mode of this phase – and learning is only possible on a basis of security, which the newly established partnership with Andromeda gives. The client in therapy learns how to unlearn the old patterns, responses, super-ego instructions, and trust the natural inner rhythms and the 'new self' to develop the appropriate order and find support from an improved contact with the collective. The creative artist does the same. He returns to Seriphos to dispose of unwanted inimical structures, learn to appreciate the sanctity of the Danae-Dictys spiritual partnership, the alternative to Danae and Polydectes, and reconnect with mother-strengths: the Danae wisdom of experience which complements the Andromeda wisdom of innocence. In Argos he seeks the truth of his elusive origins, and failing to find that truth, that illusory power, finds his own originality and power. The elusive absent grandfather leaves a space out of which the new impulse to make form grows.

The forms are then cultivated at the Larissa games on the basis of indispensable aspects of tradition and through the mysteries of craft, the ritual exercise of skill and discipline. The context of the funeral, the sense of ancestry and continuity, of celebrating a departed life, as well as the synchronicity and seeming chance associated with Acrisius's predicted death, emphasise the trans-personal dimension essential to supportive structures, which must know their own limitations. Boundaries are being newly set and affirmed as part of re-formation: the 'lineaments' that Blake saw as so necessary to the containment of powerful energies. Music and mathematics are non-verbal ritual arts of this kind, very much masculine practices. The cultivation of critical theory belongs here also. T. S. Eliot's essay: 'Tradition and the Individual Talent' (1920) is particularly relevant.

In therapy a variety of techniques will be used to assist in the re-formation. This is complex and closely bound up with the termination of the therapy, the 'funeral' in which the 'games' and rituals of therapy are the setting for separation and death, within a psychotherapeutic tradition, a craft that aims to foster new life and the integrity of the personality. Often client and therapist are as unwilling and as surprised as Perseus and Acrisius at the reality, the manner and the finality of their separation. Even though the ending is set up according to some traditional ritual, any residual ego in the therapist is likely to be violated by the client whose new strengths were unimaginable in terms of the old theories. The client may leave before the agreed date, or shift immediately to another therapist – which is 'against the rules', and unwise, but the therapist can no longer impose the rules, nor any definition of unwisdom.

The complexities implicit here, of construction, de-construction and re-construction, have been the preoccupation of linguistic and literary theoreticians for some years now, but the following enigmatic statement from the Talmud seems to place them in context, while relating also to Acrisius and Perseus:

> If the old tell you to tear down, while the young tell you to build up, you must not build up, because the destruction of the old is construction. The construction of the young is destruction.

The killing of Acrisius: death of the old form.
Re-interpretations

The skill, and the inherited awareness and acceptance of the needed death of the old, inform new creative work which inevitably, intentionally or not, deals a death-blow at the old regime, at the form which threatened tó stifle it at birth. Acrisius is hit in the 'Achilles' heel' and sometimes a work, by the very power of its complex craft, leaves a space open in itself, a vulnerability which clearly marks the weakness that has a hold unawarely on the creator. The weak spot is sometimes a signal to the artist as to where his next work lies: he will only recognise that if he has become sufficiently disidentified from the old – in other words has experienced the space left in Argos where he'd thought his identity to be.

This is signally true of male literature which often founders, like Acrisius, on its implicit male chauvinist assumptions, but cannot shed them because to acknowledge them is more than the system can bear. *Hamlet* is a case in point. The puzzling unsatisfactoriness of this powerful play lies in its basis in the patriarchal revenge-ism of the old king, the absent father. Unlike Perseus, Hamlet ends up killing everybody at the 'funeral rites' of the last scene – rites and mourning which were never adequately performed when Hamlet's father died. It is a holocaust, not a civilised ritual. The figures who correspond to Perseus's relatives all die, but the Acrisius survives as a righteous patriarchal ghost-figure to be pitied and avenged, when in fact he needed to be killed off – something Hamlet and Shakespeare, unlike Perseus, could not do. Yet by its very failure, its Achilles' heel, *Hamlet* deals a death-blow at the revenge ethic of the time. T. S. Eliot wrote a perceptive commentary on the weakness of *Hamlet*, and his own career is a striking example of the Danae–Perseus myth in action, reflecting powerfully our twentieth-century process.[13]

Perseus is an involuntary instrument of inevitable process, probably interpreting Acrisius's death as tragic accident. We know differently. D. H. Lawrence said 'Never trust the artist: trust the tale.' The myth of Danae and Perseus, which could be seen, and was doubtless told, as a patriarchal tale of a hero (half-god) and his daring exploits slaying female monsters and rescuing a helpless virgin, carries a far different truth about the death of patriarchy and the wisdom and strength of the feminine and of women. The wisdom of the myth is the knowledge of the oracle, who foretold the tale. This was then re-told and interpreted in different ways. If we want to know the 'message' of the myth, the tale, we have only to look forward to what it finally creates: Gorgophone.

The new dynasty: foundation and composition

The decision not to take over the throne of Argos but to start a new dynasty elsewhere marks the transition from learning to establishing authorship: there comes a point when one must break from traditional form, finish mourning it, move sideways and take up authority firmly, on the basis of all one has experienced, to carry out the new task from the new perspective. This is where the truly innovative originating work begins, on its own 'premises'. In a single creative project this may mean starting again, or a revision or re-working of what was done before. A new language is to be made: it is Perseus's and Andromeda's, designed to meet their needs, to communicate with one another and with the world, not the needs or expectations of the previous generation. The new language combines active and passive, thought and feeling, right- and left-brain activity, inner and outer reality, the 'bisexuality' which marks highly creative achievement. The more fundamental the work, the slower, more careful, delicate and difficult it is at this stage, but there is a strength and confidence now, a new sense of self, a confidently developing ego at work, in collaboration with its own ego-lessness. There is a firm assumption of a form that, in previous terms, was not form.

The composer Franco Donatoni[14] seems to sum up, in a different way, the work of completion, and to echo many of the pre-occupations of the myth:

It's hard to talk about the final realisation of a work. It's more like a constant coming-into-being of ideas which seek a wholeness, a roundness, while at the same time recognising the absence of a centre.

Which, put another way, means there is composition, but never total completion: 'In my end is my beginning.' The work goes on.

148

The Perseus/Andromeda strength is in knowing that: it makes possible the achievement that will know its limitations and therefore be strong. Its achievement will be Gorgophone, who is allowed to have a mind of her own.

Gorgophone and the survival of meaning

Ultimately any creative work must culminate in the feminine principle extricating itself from the unwise masculine drive to self-destruct, controlling and negating life. A project may come to an end, a poetic form may die: the poetry of life will go on. Gorgophone simply walks away from dead form. The human spirit will always do so, though there may have to be many pyres before masculine wisdom is restored sufficiently to support, not exploit human creativity and the feminine. Every work of art and healing contributes to that: these are 'divine' media, the divine presence as process. While the masculine is contracted, withdrawn, self-castrating, absent, the many-faceted feminine has to keep faith with heaven and earth in mute devotion, with tenacity, wisdom, toughness, her darkness erupting violently here and there, her pain borne responsibly without undue moralising, submitting sometimes to the corruption which she knows is part of the life process, holding on to her inner truth. Danae, Medusa, Andromeda, Gorgophone are the heroines of the Absent Father saga; the feminine in hiding, the oracle, spoke the wisdom of the creative process.

Danae, the pregnant virgin, was the creatrix who will perforce appear when needed. I append here two Danae poems, the trilogy written when the myth first took hold of me, the other as this book was coming to completion. They are explorations and models of creative process, a fulfilment of the oracle.

Danae 1980

1 Inspiration

She put
One finger of her right hand
On her clit,
And thought about liberated lesbians.

She put
Two fingers of her
Left hand
In her cunt,
And thought about departed lovers.

But the grey shades
Of the impotent men
(So many)
Seemed to want to get in,
And chill her dry.

The sun shone bright
Through her bedroom window.

She opened her legs, let in the golden warmth,
Imagined sunbeam kisses,
Labial moistness:
The entry of the orgasmic god
Bringing his energy,
Wanting her body
For its tender vibrancy,
Its ecstasy of aliveness,
The pain of its aloneness,
The passion of its humanness.
Come, god, she called out,
And I come with you . . .

For the moment
She had to be satisfied
With that.

The spirit
At least
Is willing
If we dedicate ourselves to it.

2 *Natural childbirth*

(*Acrisius*: Ill-judgment *Danae*: She who judges. The parched one)

My tyrant father
Envied my sex:
Saw me woman,
Felt life,
Unbuckled, and
Chastity
Belted me:
Seized my womb
With terror of him,
Locked me up
In hatred fear
Of my fertility.

Now
Now at the moment of birth
How shall this child get out?
No room.
I labour with him,
Knowing him from months of loving rhythm,
Wanting him:
The passion of his coming;
Longing, yet fighting in terror
The surge, the thrill;
Locking his life in the insidious prison
Of my holding muscle,
My father's No, thou shalt not
Be free.

He violates me, this male child.
Our agony
Is his raping his way out
Through my twisted, shrieking body
And my stark scream:
How shall a free child be born from a prison?

Now
He has come.
Look – I recognise him:
Son of my sun.

Lie now on my body
On my breasts:
Lie close to my heart.
The golden warmth that father'd you
Is ours now,
Healing, reconciling.
My womb moves, stirs, closes.
Our hearts beat, separate, together.

This love is wise:
It knows its origin.

When you are a man
As sure as Christ's love killed Jehovah
So you shall kill
Your grandfather.
You carry that violence in your head.
You have that knowledge of his iron hold.
You'll recognise the jailer when you meet.

You, son, shall be
The potent man that never husbanded me.

You man shall love and kill.

3 Manchild of our time

(*Perseus*: The destroyer)

Mother, I have no father.

Mother, there was that man:
Your father.
You had a father.

Mother, my right arm
Is strong:
And my head hurt
With rage I could not understand
And my eyes blind
With tears I could not understand
And I must show my strength.

My right arm freed itself
From the burden of you
With which I'm shouldered,
And flung its power:
So that I thrilled, mother,
With my body's daring
Violent thrust.
That is my beauty.

Where did I aim?
My head in an iron hold,
My eyes blind.
Did you guide my arm?
Was it not I flinging my power into space
Beneath the omniscient sun that father'd me?
I love my body and its strength.

He is dead, mother.
What does it mean?
My heart's bereft.
I think, even the god within me weeps.

I have no carnate father
To explain these things to me.

153

The spirit moves within me.
The spirit is willing
My actions.
The sun may caress, gentle, healing,
Or burn and kill with a stroke.

What is the meaning
Mother
Of the life you gave me?

Danae to Zeus

It's long ago now, but I don't forget:
The glow. Prison walls. Glamour, disbelief.
Your attitude unromantic. And crude.
You came as a golden dream, turned into
Common philanderer when in the flesh.

Yet it was love, went deep. My womb and heart
Were moved. Your skill, finesse, revealed the god.
How shy I was . . . But I'd be bolder now
If you were to come again. You won't though.
Zeus visited me, starved soul, in prison.

There's been no one else. I've seen Perseus grow
To manhood. No other: I shunned them all.
I'm frightened. Maybe soon I'll be too old
For womb-hungry passion.
                      Perhaps you don't
Even remember me. But do you keep
Watch on your son on earth? Gifted craftsman
In arts of government and sport and love.
Killer, as predicted. I do watch him.
I scan his dear features, incessantly,
Trying to figure your reality:
Grasp again the love with which we made him.

People say he has my qualities,
Is handsome, tough, and does me credit. I
Know, I fashioned him. Without your help. He
Sometimes, in a joke, calls me his goddess.

Why do they not see your spirit in him?

I want to know you still – within the flesh
My heart is an expanding emptiness.
A human can't fill this: it needs a god.

And Perseus, born of you and me, is both:
Divine and mortal, woman and man. Where's
The mature version of this our youth? We
Could come together: spirit and flesh. I
Strive to grasp your shifting meanings: the past
Elusive, future open, the golden
Dream revealed.
                         And my heart is no longer
A shy girl locked in a father's prison.

Chapter 12

The myth and body process

How does body-life manifest in a myth? It will already be apparent that there are aspects of the story which symbolise or literally describe body events like birth, menstruation, sex, digestion, muscular activity, breathing, vision, dying: these are consciously experienced. Other events offer symbols of body-states or parts of the body, such as the golden rain, the sea-chest, Medusa's snakes, the funeral pyre: they may mean different things to different people. Some events relate to involuntary unconscious processes: cell and hormone behaviour, blood-flow, brain activity, and the nervous system; only guesses and unproven theories can be offered about these and how they are made manifest in the myth. But such fancies or fantasies don't come from nowhere, and enough work has been done with dreams[1] and with visualisation and biofeed-back,[2] to suggest that body processes which are invisible and seemingly not available to our awareness are in fact sending and receiving messages through symbols, images and dreams. To be able to dialogue with one's unseen body is of inestimable value.

Since this myth is basically about the transformational healing of an initial traumatic abuse of sexual, life energy, to follow its course through progressive stages of physical change, ill- and well-being in one's own body is healing also, particularly at times of radical transition. The facilitation works both ways: attention to the body's process will enhance the progress of one's 'myth'. Attention to the development of the myth at a mental, emotional and interpersonal level will enhance the body's healing.

The modes are similar to those in the creative process.[3] The 'holding and letting go' dynamic is a basic energy pattern: cellular development is a process of accumulation, formation, death, release, birth. The behaviour of muscles is one of tension and relaxation, exercised involuntarily or with voluntary effort in time, and controlled and allowed by breathing. Holding and letting go of what is taken in, be it air or something solid, is part of the individual's self-determination. The other pattern of creativity in body-life, less willed and conscious, is more relaxed, spacial, interpersonal. Breathing is easy, withholding tensions have eased, and there is contact with other bodies and with nature. Outer rather than inner space is the concern, and the energy and rhythms are shared: they flow through touch and the other senses between individuals and the environment.

These two modes match, and are involved in, the equivalent processes of creativity and therapy.

The absent father: rigidity, spinelessness, heartlessness

The two most common manifestations of the absent father syndrome in our society are heart-disease and lower back pain. The latter afflicts a high percentage of the adult population, reflecting a basic Western ungroundedness. The legs of a person who is well grounded on mother earth can take the weight of the body through a relaxed pelvis, and the father-support from behind the person who walks out to face the world manifests in a confident lower back and an unstrained forward movement. Where this support is missing there is a lack of backbone, a sense of spinelessness – this is compensated for by excessive spinal rigidity and a tight pelvis and shoulders, part of the inhibiting control of sexual and anal behaviour which further blocks the energy flow downward. Following the absent father may also mean a manic, anxious driven forward movement. All this produces back-ache and the whole is compounded by restriction of movement, lack of free exercise, slavery to machines, too much sitting, and the collapsed dejection of slumped shoulders which have been too tense, taken too many burdens and are not 'standing up to' the oppressors. This chest collapse restricts the breathing: the heart is starved of oxygen, over-stressed, the feelings repressed, the body uncared for, over-worked:

ultimately heart-disease may develop. This is a manic-depressive body.

The depressed body is Danae: confined and unfree, unable to move outwards and forwards, her sexuality locked up, dejected, unsupported, unloved. And her heart also locked up by, and against, her father, her breathing restricted by her imprisoning environment.

The manic body, Acrisius, is ungrounded, unable to give in to time and process: he must be doing. But in middle age he is anxious about his potency. An ungrounded man of his age, either rigidly slim or laxly pot-bellied, has reduced sexual motility: the presence of an attractive daughter is a challenge. Threatened by the oracle's wisdom and its suggestion of impotence and ageing, he lets his penis, rather than his heart, rule his head, and then he rules from that head. His eyes do not weep for the loss of his daughter, nor for himself; they become unseeing, non-receptive, only directive. And his head is set in its long-cultivated inflexibility: as we saw in chapter 1, he is the exposed head of the family body, so he is stiff-necked.

Within Acrisius's rigid regime these are the usual body-states. They are familiar to many of us: in time they can become chronic diseases (Harrison 1986).

Zeus: the stimulation of energy, sexuality and breathing

The escape from this regime, from the ills inherent in its stressful way of life, can only come through love of one's own body and the release of bound energy. Zeus's visit answers the body's need for that release, for life. The idea comes that creative change is possible and there is hope for an escape from depression: new vitality can be generated in this body. Sex offers that release, with or without the actual making of another new life. Zeus's visit may be either an occasion of sexual encounter or of auto-eroticism (see *Danae 1980* above). The freeing of sexual energy relaxes and stirs the heart, stimulates the imagination and the breathing (= inspiration). But since the body is still ruled by Acrisius control, this single event will be only a frustrated beginning, giving birth to an energy (Perseus) which will have to grow and become aggressive enough in time to break down the body's complex of tensions and holding. In the specific area of sexuality, the control pattern set up in adolescence will be tighter when the sexual feelings coming from the parent ware strong and strongly denied. As long as the mutual attraction is a guilty secret, the father's incestuous hold over his daughter remains. The same is true of mother and son. Zeus's arrival is a vital beginning, however, to unlocking the tensions and giving back to the person possession of their own body.

The golden rain may be semen: it may be vaginal lubrication stimulated by masturbation. It could be cells, hormones, messages from the brain which is fantasising impregnation and heart-warming sunlight. Then through orgasm there is a release of breathing: the rib-cage will seem less imprisoning. Zeus brings in air, gives the vital inspiration.

Masturbation, self-loving, plays a significant part in the reclaiming of one's sexuality – particularly for women, many of whom achieve a more satisfying orgasm on their own than with an unimaginative partner whose presence is little better than absence. It is a self-containing but inevitably self-limiting activity. The arguments about clitoral and vaginal (and anal) orgasm are relevant here. An erect clitoris is a kind of Perseus: a woman's mini-penis engendered in the absence of another's penis. The clitoral orgasm is powerful but doesn't plumb the depths of the vaginal/rectal 'Medusa cave', the place of deep feminine receptive need, a place not only of pleasure and ecstasy but also of anger, blood and woundedness associated with menstruation, defecation and childbirth. A full head-to-toe orgasm, as described by Reich (1942), which releases the whole body energy, hasn't been achieved. Danae's immature experience of masturbating or of her 'one-night stand' with her 'fancy man' is not enough to release the deeply repressed creative sexuality, so it remains depressed throughout the foetal life of Perseus, his birth and growth, until he releases it in confronting and freeing the Medusa: the numbed cervix of the womb.

The feeling of being pregnant produces a state of bliss, excitement, devotion and self-centredness that immediately alters the body energy to a more vibrant, hopeful self-possession: the first step in giving up possession by the repressive father. Women who have already had children feel many of the symptoms of real pregnancies in this phase of a creative embarking on a new project which leads to renewed life.

Gestation, birth, post-natal depression: the imprinted self-creation process

The first stages of re-production of the self during a period of transition will be a replay of the individual's birth-process. The experience of child and mother re-produces itself in the body, through energy movements, in sex, digestion and excretion, and menstruation. Breathing, heart-beat and blood-pressure are affected appropriately. I can only point to some of the phenomena suggested by the birth of Perseus and the sea-chest journey: individuals will recognise other cognate experiences. Primal and bioenergetic therapies put people closely in touch with these body memories through techniques of regression and abreaction. But for anyone going through a transitional life-crisis, puzzling and alarming physical events occur spontaneously (Sheehy, 1976). Some are undoubtedly a replay of the birth experience, like fits of claustrophobia (people often curl up in a foetal posture and hide in a corner), acute panic, severe headaches, convulsions and breathing difficulties.

The womb-life of Perseus is that of a baby within a depressed mother whose womb reproduces the prison that confines her: a sad, toxic environment (Lake 1987). But Danae's hopefulness is there, and the urge to freedom: determination, or defiance. And this is the basic body experience of the person embarking on transformation: a mixture of depression, mistrust, and confident excitement, felt usually in the stomach and bowels.

The birth process was described in chapter 3, and more of the experience emerges later in the Medusa's cave. The excessive holding caused by Acrisius control over the pelvic area means a difficult birth. But the myth gives Perseus several opportunities to play out the pattern and change it, as he clears the trauma in successive experiences: the same is true in the body's progress, working through different layers and degrees of tension to release frozen pain and energy.

The first 'replay' in the sea-chest is a characteristic post-natal situation. A baby's 'three-month colic', a mother's depression, are an adaptation to the new life but within that a clearing of traumatic pre-natal and perinatal experiences. The 'confinement' is re-enacted and all the suppressed fear, anger, repulsion, distress and loneliness re-surfaces – only to be confined and enclosed yet again by

Acrisius's rejection: social disapproval of the expression of such feelings, which is internalised along with them. The sea-chest journey manifests in restricted breathing, anxiety, depressed energy, nausea and vomiting phobia: fear that one's violent desire to escape the new mother-baby tie may 'rock the boat', fear of the power of the oceanic: the anger and need, hormonal imbalances, vibratory streamings in the body: Poseidon's deep turbulences which are without and within us and seem to threaten to swallow us up. These are features of post-natal depression and of transitional life-crises.

Perseus is the new heart of the enterprise, and the heart is protected throughout this journey. Though anxiety threatens, his system is now sufficiently separate from Danae's that he can develop his own strength to survive: his heart is 'encouraged' by her love. The body has new heart and energy even though it still tenses against the upsurge of unacceptable feelings.

The sea-chest journey represents hibernation also: the enclosed carrying of new life through the dark winter months. Many people experience winter in their bodies as a time of contraction, an inevitable dampening of energy. To this one may have to submit, and there are needed times of emotional contraction and hibernation also.

It is probable, too, that this is a phase of the menstrual cycle, whose stages are gone through in the myth. The ovum was born in Argos: Zeus's golden shower the pituitary hormones which cause the egg to form in the follicle. Now it is travelling along the fallopian tube, and ovulation will take place in the 'white' stage at Seriphos – the maternal-reproductive phase of the cycle. Since Danae is *not* impregnated there, the experience in the Medusa's cave is of pre-menstrual tension followed by blood-flow, the shedding of the womb-lining (Medusa's body) and release of energy: the 'red' phase – sexual-creative (Shuttle and Redgrove 1986).

The sea-chest may also be the lower bowel and bladder, the excretory system carrying its urine and faeces, containing it through precarious disturbances until it can be expelled on to suitable ground. The anal-urethral control and rejection by Acrisius causes tight holding and repression of the need to let go. The wetness of tears, the weeping of urine, is held back. This is the excretory system paralleling the birth experience.

Seriphos will be the upper bowel and stomach where intake from
the outer environment is managed, and sickness is more evident and
accessible: but a further descent to the enclosed lower bowel will be
necessary in the Medusa's cave to deal with hidden self-destructive
processes.

Seriphos: socialisation of energy

With the emergence from the sea-chest's fearful darkness, and
reassurance that it can survive the turbulence of released emotions,
the body now breathes more freely, feels born-again, is able to
stand on supportive ground, stand its ground. It moves from the
closedness, energy held and hunched inside its own skin, and
expands its boundaries, negotiates protection from others who
understand its needs and maintains self-protection also (as Danae),
while its Perseus energy is nurtured and allowed to live, to flourish
in comparative freedom in the safe setting of a relaxed grounded
body.

But the memory of past suffering and repressed rebelliousness,
which has now 'gone underground' is there during this period, and
as the Perseus energy grows, and becomes potentially creative:
sexual, aggressive, socially outrageous, dangerous, so the old
mechanisms come back to deal with it, and the depressive,
idealising mother and controlling and disempowering impatient
father are in conflict and conspiracy, tying up the new energy.

This triad is an energetic complex most bodies live with, and few
in our society are comfortable with this kind of socialisation. It is a
superficial manipulation of the deeper instinctual feeling life of the
body, its dark Argos and sea-chest knowledge and its sexuality and
fertility. Holding on and letting go become acute problems as we
try to free ourselves from stressful body tensions which are holding
out against the realisation of our repressed energies. The Danae/
Polydectes conflict registers in increasing ill-health which has
become an obsession with symptoms and with the pain caused by
the stifling of energies. There is a resultant loss of caring and
responsibility for the life-energy in the body itself, for Perseus and
his raison d'être. Only when we venture, as Perseus does, to go into
the fundamental nature of the sickness, confront its deeper meaning
and the destructive deathliness in it, have we hope of health. And

fundamentally challenging it is to the whole stressful lifestyle imposed by society.

The kinds of symptomatic illness involved are usually those in which intake from outside is resisted, lest it either release, or totally suppress, an eruption of unwelcome deep feelings or body energies. Danae will not let in Polydectes: sexual and heart conditions result from this closure. The digestive system resists intake or proper assimilation of food, lest it over-stimulate: 'upset' the lower bowel. Bronchitis and asthma mark the inability to take in deep breaths which will revitalise the body. Soon the whole system is anxious, self-obsessed and exhausted with its struggle. The energy-flow, and the canalisation of powerful energy into appropriate activity, is blocked. But the anger ultimately takes over and either intelligently – with Athena's wisdom – resolves to look deeper for a cure, or dangerously turns on itself in destructive self-damaging ways: a near-suicidal entry into severe disease (our inner Polydectes sending Perseus to meet his fate) which forces us to find our will to live and our understanding of how to live – makes us confront the Medusa. This scenario is familiar to cancer-sufferers, and cancer is very much related to the suppression of emotional energy, anger in particular.

The heart and spirit of Perseus and the wisdom of Athena find a way to face the blocked vitality which will heal and renew life – which means coming to terms with the darker forces, the disgraced aspects of human energy, which turn sour in the body if they are denied or disowned, and coming to terms with death.

Excavating the Medusa's cave; purging and dissolution of destructive sickness: release of vital energy

The bodily discharge and dispersion of blocked feelings in primal and bioenergetic therapy, or in co-counselling, Gestalt therapy and psychodrama, or through acupuncture or Rolfing, are the most powerful ways of dealing with Medusa sicknesses caused by suppression of energy; the first releases achieved this way are as dramatic as Perseus's severing her head. Subsequently these therapeutic experiences will need integrating (as signified by the rest of the myth). When such levels of body experiencing are inaccessible other therapies and treatments will be used, and sometimes a slow putrefaction process must be borne in the body and the final release by a determined Perseus will be at an emotional level, a resolution to discard the hold of the corrupted body, of sickness itself, as a needed condition (Harrison, 1986).

The Medusa state and its morbid pathology was explored in some detail in chapters 5 and 6. To summarise: she represents all that sickness of body which is caused by the envious mind's conflict with the 'dark god' of our baser feelings (Athena's conflict with Poseidon), the mind's attack on its own body (Medusa) when it has been taken over by those 'baser' feelings, the mind's envious attack and discrediting of the healing power of the body itself (Medusa's snakes and blood).

Thus the Danae/Polydectes conflict – of outward symptoms, between mortals, is found, in the underworld cave, to be a deep conflict between gods – fundamental attitudes to the body – a crisis of the soul which has been played out in mortals' bodies. In this earth-spirit medium of the innermost unseen body the corruption is a critical life-and-death transformation. Poison has been absorbed from the outside: the system can neither expel nor properly digest it: vital energy is paralysed: others recoil from the Medusa's repulsive sourness. She needs to die to give birth but cannot. Cancer is a condition in which cells refuse to die.

The process is self-perpetuating: the orthodox medical profession too much refuses to accept the mystery of death, and the need to find meaning through pain. It blocks entry to the Medusa's cave with tranquillisers and symptom-suppressing drugs. These in their turn become poisonous, and the doctor can become the Medusa, the corrupted mothering healer, who paralyses us.

All the conditions experienced in the Argos prison and the sea-chest journey which were repressed by fear and the need to survive are now recalled with a vengeance, and the Perseus energy fights for its life against the Medusa who is a perversion of the mother and the body. She envies his life and growth and seems to curse him. (It is common for children of cancer sufferers to feel 'cursed' by the parent: destined to die of the disease.) This condition of envy was explored in chapter 5. It does come through the head: the 'evil eye', but also, more subtly, in its disdainfulness, through the nose. The envious state, in particular of intellectual destructiveness, manifests, according to the bio-energeticist Robert Olins,[4] in the face: the nose, which we 'turn up' as we smell odorous others, sniff, and snort out attacking breath dismissively.

The head that Perseus sees in reflection and dare not see face to face, the mythical monstrous head, is powerfully associative because we are so much 'in our heads', and relate so little with the rest of our bodies. From birth on, the less happy the body relationship is to mother and to others, the more fixated and dominating the head relationship.

The eyes can mediate every kind of emotional transaction: control, distance and closeness, fear, hatred, rejection, seduction. The body cannot lie, but the eyes and ocular interchange can certainly deceive, manipulate. Pain, too, or the choice to withdraw, is visible in the eyes, which pull back from looking. This is absence, and the more fixed this schizoid non-seeing stare, the more threatened are those who seek contact with the person.

Headaches, migraine, stiffnecks, have origins in very early traumas, which are restimulated at critical points in later life, particularly where anger and fear are being suppressed. (Cranial osteopathy works on this assumption.) In the birth the baby's head feels enormous to itself and may be stuck, seemingly endlessly, while the expulsive energy is driven into it and blocked, and the jaw and neck jammed fast. Any subsequent repression of anger, of oral aggression, in a situation of frustration may produce the headache or migraine[5] and the stiff-necked stubbornness that will not give way to the life-aggressive urge within. This is repeated at the breast or bottle wherever there is conflict: the baby's anger at being over- or under-fed, inadequately held, results in paralyzing conflict at the back of the neck as it goes toward and pulls away from mother or food at one and the same time.

To look on the Medusa's head calls up all these old horrors. One woman felt herself, as the Medusa, to be *in utero*, trying to get out, with a tangled mess (of snakes – pubic hair?) around her head. All the energy was in her head which she felt needed cutting off at the neck.

Tension at the nape of the neck can also be an attempt to control and fixate the vision, or to evade the fixation required by intent and unrelaxed watching or staring. One is not being receptive to impressions, seeing what is there (as is possible by using Perseus's mirror), but too actively and narrowly looking.

The intra-uterine environment is recalled in the Medusa's cave, and commonly reproduced in the digestive system. The intake by the foetus of maternal distressful poison is life-threatening: the baby's system has to work hard to convert it: this Perseus does. But if there is too much poison the foetus exists in a state of paranoia (Lake 1987) which may draw it, in later life, time and again, to distressful and poisonous persons and practices, like the Medusa, until the stomach, the whole body and the person's world reproduce the closed-circuit toxic womb: constipation, ulcers, acid indigestion, and resentful bitterness. Killing the Medusa means breaking through and out of this womb, and, having cut the cord, escaping the persecutory placenta (the pursuing Gorgons?) which implies breaking from a bad environment.

At an unconscious level the cord itself, the vital vehicle of dependency, is remembered (Mott 1959) and probably represented here by the three Gorgons – Medusa the single vein through which comes the mother's blood, often experienced as threateningly invasive and quasi-phallic in its power, and the two sisters, the two arteries through which the foetus returns its waste product to the placenta. These arteries too are experienced as potentially aggressive, attacking the environment.

At the birth and cord-cutting, our attitudes to blood, blood-loss, blood-connection and severance of body tissues and blood-vessels are all central to this crisis of connection with, and separation from, the maternal, and from the body's hold on us. The Gorgon's blood can heal – and Pegasus is born from it. Blood is a mystery, a wonderful organic substance, but menstrual taboos and fears of the death-dealing mother have turned awe into fascinated repulsion and an obsession with murder and violation (Shuttle and Redgrove, 1986).

Perseus is the right arm that cuts the cord. Being male, he personifies the left-brain principle, and he is his mother's right arm in the outside world. The cord-cutting is usually experienced in the unconscious as a masculine activity: the guilt-feelings around cutting the cord are internalised in the right arm, which may therefore remorsefully pull back its own full energy (Laing 1976). At the same time the shock of sudden disconnection from mother's pulse-beat manifests in the heart area which immediately contracts: there is a 'hardening of the heart' which never entirely leaves us and keeps us from overly merging with m/others. Such hardening makes it possible for Perseus to use his right arm incisively: the use of the mirror distances, disconnects him from the seductive all-embracing placenta/vagina. After the severance, the body breathes for itself and establishes its own metabolic system, as Pegasus and Perseus will. The presence, of an ill-willed, shallow-breathing person can poison and suffocate us, and to break free of the relationship one may have to harden one's heart.

The right arm is an expression of masculine potency. Perseus is asserting his virility and destroying the malign force that seeks to castrate him. He himself represents the penis. The Medusa, with her serpentine 'femme fatale' quality, can stiffen and paralyse the penis to what feels like a vulnerable rigid brittleness (phallic qualities evinced by Acrisius and Polydectes). Phallocentric energy is easily isolated from the rest of male body energy. In that sense the caring father (the whole body) is often absent from the son's outwardly directed activities, and the 'son' may then be very exposed as Perseus is to the 'vagina dentata' which can swallow him up. The penis is often betrayed and rejected by the person in charge of it.

The loss of a right arm or of right-arm power is frequently associated with the Medusa presence: the existence of malign forces that men cannot come to terms with – Ahab in *Moby Dick* has lost his to the white whale. In *The White Hotel* the character Richard Lionheart (mentioned in chapter 8 p. 84) has lost his right arm in combat. The history of Ravel's piano concerto for the left hand, written in the context of World War One horrors he could not cope with, is also relevant.[6] Loss of this body member can lead to impotence and defeatism, but the left arm can compensate. Its activity may be 'sinister', 'gauche', but also more flexibly feminine, less brutal. In mid-life and subsequent crises, such as the climacteric, men may become impotent in their work-sphere. They have to accept a more right-brain, left-arm way of living – but may first have to use the right arm to cut the ties that bind them to the activity they need to outgrow. The menopausal male often turns the menopausal female into the Medusa: he needs to see, in the mirror-shield, what he has done; how he has projected his own crisis on to her, and misinterpreted her sexual energy, her power and maturity, as he has misinterpreted his own.

I have referred to the way the menstrual cycle is represented in the myth up to this point. It is at this crucial stage of onset of menstruation that woman's sexual energy is transmuted into spiritual, creative energy, beyond childbearing. This has far-reaching implications for evolution (suggested by Pegasus) and is archetypally represented by dark goddesses of transformation like the Medusa. Shuttle and Redgrove (1986) explore this whole area of the body-spirit transition in detail.[7] I have suggested in chapter 7 (p. 73) some ideas about this evolutionary transformation.

Pegasus and the freeing of high energy

The birth of Pegasus, the release of energy from holding, as described in chapter 7, is always accompanied by a dramatic change in breathing. This replicates the original birth experience. The chest (the cave) ceases to be constrictive and suddenly there is space to expand the breath and great relief after the spastic holding. Where the breathing itself was acutely constricted, as in asthma, the diaphragmatic spasm may be cleared by vomiting. Or one may be spitting and vomiting up the acid contents of the poisoned stomach, the feelings swallowed: fear and repulsion and stress, and soured lovesickness. Generally the obsessive frown of the depressed head (again a birth memory) disappears, and energy flows outwards. The body's frightened rigidity dissolves: jaw, shoulders, lower back and pelvis relax and are able, with the limbs, to move with rhythm and freedom. There is often a strong impulse to get out of doors and move: run, walk, break free, sing, dance. The body begins to feel more whole, and real, as it expands its boundaries.

This transition can be consciously facilitated by expanding and deepening the breathing. Though breathing blocks and tensions have developed, from birth onwards, the average person can always feed themselves more oxygen, and ordinary exercise, or special therapeutic exercises, will improve this. The equation posited by Fritz Perls (1946) – *anxiety = excitation without oxygen* – is an invaluable one to remember in all circumstances of bodily and emotional stress.

However, with the Pegasus release comes the memory of the initial terrifying fall into gravity, so there will be a fear that one's body, the womb-world of muscular tensions, will fall apart, and a fear of getting 'carried away', of excitement, giddiness. There may be hyperventilation until the system adapts to fuller breathing: the new-born energy will need grounding. Unfamiliar vibratory stream-ings or unfocused light-headedness can accompany this release and sometimes there is a reactive tensing up, a retreat back into contraction and depression.

There may be a tendency to diarrhoea, after constipation, which causes anxiety, as does vomiting: fear of loss of body contents. After premenstrual tension too there comes elation but also a collapse into tiredness: the blood-loss is both a relief and a draining.

Likewise the sexual release into full orgasm, in which the body's energy is freed, is an ecstatic experience but can feel shattering and draining, particularly after a period of much holding. Grounding here is achieved by the close contact with the sexual partner, while in the 'afterglow', the energy is allowed to flow evenly and infuse the whole body. This is another reason why masturbation may be unsatisfying, when the full orgasm is being avoided because it cannot be grounded in another's body. This parallels the close contact needed with mother's body after birth; both these situations meet heart needs also: they are pacemakers, restoring the rhythmic balance of the breathing in a love embrace. For Perseus this grounding comes later: landing on Andromeda's ground and meeting her in sexual love. Pegasus foreshadows this, soaring upward, then coming to ground voluntarily on the Muses' territory, again a symbol of masturbation and its connection with art.

The individual Pegasus experience nurtures the imagination and challenges us, as it does Perseus, to take proper charge of our bodies. In life-transitions with severe somatic symptoms, there may be a disturbance of the ability to walk, as long-held pelvic and leg tensions are released: the flexibility and breathing must be exercised, the feet well grounded, to enable more energy to infuse the legs and help them recontact the earth. The same applies to arms and hands whose aggressive instincts have long been held in. The eyes seem to lose their ability to focus, for they have been fixed in the dry-eyed Medusa stare and will now need to shed tears, to relieve the sorrow, envious anger and fear that has been held in. They then can re-focus and look at the world with 'different eyes'. Fear itself, which has paralysed the body, may surface in involuntary trembling and fits of panic. Fear and excitement are closely allied: the energy charge needs to be allowed to find both an outward channel of release and a grounding and containment.

The Pegasus state is a model: free-flowing and balanced energy: a healthy exercise of great physical power that is in one's own charge, a combination of weight and lightness, of animal and spirit, a freedom that is not interfered with by other, earth-bound, forces. This winged state is not attainable by mortal human-bodies which have moved from the horse stage in another evolutionary direction and remain earth-bound. But we can come nearer the ideal than our timid minds sometimes think, and stretch our imagination by stretching our bodies. Systems of body re-alignment, such as Tai Chi, bio-energetics, Alexander and Feldenkrais techniques, osteopathy, acupuncture, postural integration, are designed to bring us near to an ideal balancing of energy. The Yin and Yang of the Andromeda/Perseus marriage is the human version of Pegasus's 'androgynous' energy: the Larissa games suggest the discipline of those re-balancing practices.

Perseus and Andromeda: reclaiming the frightened body: integration, integrity and the power of healing

When Perseus is 're-born' he must find again the young mother he originally came to after his birth, the mother of the sea-chest, and work through whatever was unhealthy and ungrounding in that initial relationship, which is transacted through feeding and excretion. In the early days these were major concerns for survival. The baby's and mother's stomachs carried the memory of the umbilical relationship in Argos. Perseus, this second time around, has just come from the sickness of the Medusa's cave. Now there must be adjustment again to a measured voluntarised oral intake, and a different relationship with the source of nourishment. The basic conflicts are played out in the digestive and the sexual system: Perseus and Andromeda between them transcend the illness and go forward to health.

Free intake, free defecation, and the high, often orgasmic excitement of passionate feeding at the breast (both mother and baby are sexually aroused – baby boys often have erections) can, like the Pegasus state, be both enjoyable and frightening. Parental attitudes to food, to excreta, to vomiting and the passing of wind, up or down, to sexual excitement, will set off control mechanisms which then work forwards or backwards to inhibit proper digestion. The mother, once again, will be experienced as the

171

dangerous Medusa who poisons the stomach and teases only to deprive or de-sex.

Andromeda, however, carries a different energy from that of the Danae/Medusa figure. She is not enclosed and trapped in her depression; she is openly appealing, and available to be met by Perseus. He is no longer the son being dominated by mother's feelings in the sea-chest and the Medusa's cave, but separate and able to see her plight and help her. Now we have Perseus intelligence, on the basis of body experience from which he has achieved Pegasus detachment, able to deal with body crises, see their meaning, and assist healing. He has learned how to adjust his view of woman and the body. Their ultimate coming together will mark the transition from orality to sexuality, and thence to spirituality.

It is the handling and grounding of fear and excitement, of 'hysterical' illness, that is the basic need here. Andromeda herself resembles the newborn: naked, exposed, by a mother who has doubtless boasted that she and her daughter are clean and dry and decent, unlike the wet sea-nymphs who belong to Poseidon's realm of the lower instincts.

The she-monster rising from Poseidon's depths is the intemperate impatience and disgusting greed which wants to devour everything, swallowing without tasting, upset the system and cause the helpless body to disgrace itself with vomit or faeces (or, for a man, emissions of semen). The fright of this monster in us will itself cause loss of control. This kind of crisis, based on fear of both regulated and unregulated feeding, manifests in chronic indigestion, addictions, and anorexia/bulimia – the latter conditions most common in 'princesses': daughters of affluent families, and sometimes producing a life-and-death Andromeda situation. The association of anorexia with menstrual disturbance is reflected in the adult woman's fear of disintegration through sudden loss of body contents in menstruation or childbirth; as well as the draining loss of her milk when she feeds her child. She herself is the discarded placenta, suddenly emptied body or drained breast, and the monster perhaps the life-force which overtakes and kills a woman in childbirth or exhausts her energy as she nurtures others.

Cassiopeia's beautiful daughter is bound to own the life-and-death gut knowledge, the potential she-monster, in a woman's body that is liable to overthrow all the taboos and cosmetic vanities that try to conceal it. Once it is owned it can be taken charge of, rather than plastered over. And Cassiopeia is not only in the glamorous film-star league: she exists in the women's movement also, wherever taboos and cosmetic manoeuvres try to suggest a clean and decent image of feminist woman.

Sexual greed and promiscuity parallel oral greed: they too upset the balance of energy in the body and the sexuality then cannot become creative. Women can become prey to their own exaggerated sexual needs, as well as men's, because of their fixed status as sexual objects (to be devoured) or mothers, the restriction of their mobility and creativity.

Heart, mind and sexual desire are being brought together in Perseus, whose previous experiences, confronting in the Medusa's cave the fear that split them apart in his grandfather and mother, leave him breathing more wholly and steadily with an integrating patient Pegasus rhythm. Athena's wisdom has encouraged him to conceptualise and symbolise. The masculine discriminatory sense will help the feminine, the body, regulate her intake, oral or genital, so that her own greed won't overburden her system. This is the integration process: it is related to integrity in an emotional sense (as also in systems theories and artistic accomplishment). So Perseus's careful assurance calms Andromeda's hysteria: she takes hold of her own body strength and together they cut the monster and those who evoked it down to size. The fear discharged and the excitement grounded now in reality, and in one another's bodies, they will begin to set up a healthier regime. A marriage of this kind can develop in an individual person's body, when they begin truly to love and trust their body instead of rejecting or fearing it, and are prepared to be patient with it and give it time to heal. So mind and body, body and soul are in a creative relationship. This new personality does not keep splitting itself but nurtures its wholeness. To Perseus, Andromeda is a beautiful nakedly exposed and distressed soul as well as a body. He begins to appreciate in her the power of the earth-principle and of moon-consciousness: the goddess who is spirit-in-matter, and for whom the will to live and the will to die are equally acceptable. She only becomes terrified when that knowledge, which is her life-blood, is being wrenched away from her, and her power to follow it denied her. There can be no successful mind–body relationship without the acceptance that the body has its own knowledge.

Seriphos, Argos, Larissa. The quest for the original wound: restoring the presence of the body: the nature of balance in time

As in the creative process outlined in the previous chapter, the return to Seriphos and Argos, and the dénouement at Larissa, are part of the unlearning and relearning the body has to do in order to reform itself. Seriphos is the place of pre-puberty and adolescence where socialising patterns of holding and release of energy were established: the management of excitement, ambition, display, protectiveness. In adolescence this focuses on sexuality. Ideally then one is encouraged to walk upright with ease, swing the hips, show one's external sexual features with pride and one's vulnerability without cringing, while good breathing brings an attractive vitality to the eyes and colour. In his return to Seriphos Perseus kills off the control system of Polydectes that sought to suppress, jettison and destroy his sexuality or make it stagnate. Proximity to Polydectes's own aroused and controlled sexual energy must have dampened the energy of Perseus. The older man probably breathed short, held his breath in anger, being constantly frustrated by Danae, had high blood pressure and suffered a heart attack at the sight of Perseus returning with the severed head! – the overweight middle-aged man whose anxious system can't take a sudden return of sexual energy and dies during intercourse . . . intercourse with his Medusa. No longer is either Perseus's or Polydectes's sexuality a threat to Danae, who is safe in her bond with Dictys, and Perseus's liberated, freely breathing sexual energy can now be met by Andromeda. But there are deeper controls: the depressive withdrawn Danae – the discouraged heart – still threatens to dampen his and Andromeda's spirit and deaden their vitality unless he can restore it to his body's sexual aliveness. The depression and discouragement is about the absent father: the unseen control systems whose influence he cannot assess, and the want of male support for his identity as a male. So he must go with Danae to Argos to undo the negative conditioning of his birth: the influence of the grandfather he never met. He is drawn to deal with the patterns of anal control, and control of heart and breathing that affected Danae's body when she was carrying and giving birth to him – to deal with that basic depression of his vital energy and existence.

174

Through anal control the super-ego, and patriarchy, maintains its power: this is the earliest socialisation, geared to products, not process, its spiritual power obsessed with the shameful body, its ego busy controlling time and rhythm and breathing with mechanical inhumanity. Prevalent diseases of the bowel and rectum: colitis, piles, irritable bowel syndrome, are the result of the stresses of a work-life which treats people as machines, and a religion which rejects their bodies. Male control aims to take over the threatening features of the birth (and death) process, and reproduces its own anal version of the vaginal event. Vagina and anus are close, and share the same muscle tensions, so Acrisius's anal patterns imposed on Danae will affect her vaginal and pelvic patterns of tension and they will be carried after the birth in Perseus's head, pelvis and anus to determine his anal and sexual activity.

To get into direct contact with the original male connection has dangers for Perseus. Without any civilising control over Acrisius, the powerful patriarch, instead of lovingly embracing his grandson's body, may 'bugger' him. The homosexual connection through anal intercourse is the only way men can physically simulate the act of impregnation followed by ejection of a foetal or fecal 'product'. The potential beauty of the sexual pleasure achieved is then shadowed by the vagina-envy potential – which is doubtless responsible for the extreme degradation of some promiscuous male homosexual practice: a shitty debasement of sex and the body and a mockery of the beauty of sexual relating. The fineness of homosexual relating is possible at the civilised Larissa games, but in Argos Perseus and Acrisius dare not trust themselves or one another. Perseus will not recover there his self-confidence as a man: so his body, with Acrisius's evasion and rejection of him, remains wounded in its maleness. This unhealed wound reflects the sickness of the 'dirty tricks' male political world, with its patriarchal anal-fixated degradation of creative relating: how can Perseus be a man in such a world? Small wonder he must still be as depressed as the Danae who accompanies him to Argos: he, and she, are still in thrall to the elusive Acrisius who can make a fool of him.

At this point in the body's 'unlearning' process, sometimes in the therapeutic setting, all seems hopeless: the miseries of colitis or a nervous bowel are that one cannot control the anal-urethral activity, nor can one accept the original means of control, yet there seems to be no imaginable alternative. Contact is lost, numbed, between mind and that part of the body (Perls 1946). The head cannot work out a method, for it has been 'brainwashed' by patriarchal control. Shame takes over: anger and life-aggression, asserting one's self, cannot be expressed because no one is there to receive or contain them. One has arrived at the base-line of responsibility for one's own life and self, one's process and self-management. By what clock should one regulate and measure out one's life? The anus is the tail-end of the body, where life goes out. People who mourn another's death sometimes feel they may expel them in defecating. One may lose one's life through dysentery, or contamination by faeces. Acrisius and Perseus share these masculine fears of loss of control.

But the visit to Argos is beset by secrets and the silence of Danae. The truth eludes Perseus because taboos and the wrong values have sent him in the wrong direction: to the patriarchal issue of anal control. Like Parsifal, he does not know what question to ask, and as with Parsifal the taboo subject is menstrual blood (Shuttle and Redgrove 1986). Danae has an inner clock, a cyclical, rhythmic awareness of process that encompasses death and life, loss and gain, despair and joy. This could pace him. She is silent because she has no words for menstrual wisdom, its connection to the oracle and to Zeus, its cosmic rhythms, its power to combine sex and spirit, tension and release. Acrisius depressed that wisdom, denied her bleeding, the mark of her fertility, locked her up, keeping incestuous possession, declaring the blood-connection to be through men, patrilineal, established through anal control.

So Perseus becomes the lone hero struggling in an isolated body obsessed with the control of digestion and defecation. A woman may experience it in the same way. Menstrual matters have low priority, are 'cursed', and the significance of their rhythm, their fund and well of creativity, ignored. Trust in that rhythm enhances the body's healing of itself.

However, the cycle is there, silent, like the women accompanying Perseus, present. In his physical proximity to Andromeda he will begin to be influenced by the cycle and begin to trust his body to establish its own rhythms and inner clock: its patterns of activity and repose, loss and gain, effort and relaxation, holding and letting go. *The body knows far more about its own life and death than the conscious Perseus mind knows. Andromeda knows this.* The knowledge may come through in dreams, the realm of Zeus in the brain. It was to that knowledge that Danae surrendered when

Perseus was conceived. The combination of Perseus control and Andromeda surrender will deal with the body's problem of time-bound creativity. What Perseus understands ultimately (and he is the symbolising principle) is that the carnate father who tries to annul the threatening sexual wisdom of woman has to be replaced by a fantasy father, Zeus, who is a product of the right brain, the only place that feminine wisdom can manifest and inseminate herself when she is desperate to survive. That is the secret of his virgin birth.

Danae can only mention it: she must suppress the bitter uncleared load of incestuous feeling she has swallowed, the anger, despair, distress of her own history in her stomach. She does not vomit it up, but keeps her mouth shut, hardly breathing, holding on to the father inside her, unable to expel him. So untold injustice is swallowed and adds to our gastric acidity as we ruminate bitterly on past wrongs.

But Perseus is much further on in his awareness and learning and will not collude with Danae's tight-lipped suffering that threatens to retard the process of healing. And he has Andromeda's awareness in close contact. When he knows that Argos is a dead-end place of suffocation he takes them all away into the open air, breathing regularly, mouth open, yawning, stretching, allowing the body to be infused again with oxygen and the cleansing spirit of life, the inspiration of Zeus. For the spiritual father inside him, unlike the father inside Danae, is the air that can be taken in and expelled at will.

Our conscious Perseus experience, then, in returning to Argos, is of finding and losing at once, discovering the limits of our body's power. We look for the source of control, the author of the pattern, father or mother who determined our body-life, only to discover how elusive an original influence they are. The journey, even the psycho-analytic journey, to the past takes place in the present, and arrives nowhere, or now-here. The process of digestion and excretion is within our means to determine in the present (Perls 1946). The cycle of loss and wounding and renewal experienced in menstruation is present. Though history has affected us, wounded us, given us incurable malfunctions of the body's system, we can take charge of the system and its disabilities, listen to its messages and rhythms, and build up a diet and a regularity in partnership with it.

177

It is then we come up against our own basic helplessness, and that of both Acrisius and Danae, and discover that their power to have complete control over us, and our own power of control, was always an illusion. Holding faeces back is a sad attempt to hold on to the past, similar to holding back an unborn child. Equally we find ourselves not wanting to let go of the super-ego, the supposedly omnipotent authority that ruled us, saved us from that loss and from the shame and guilt of messing ourselves up.

The attitude is compulsive, anxious about 'waste'. Time mustn't be wasted – all is stress. It is a question of pace. Recognition of this is where revaluation and re-formation of one's life begins, i.e. the place where 'it' ends.

Our faeces are our 'waste product' and we need to know whether our life experience has been a waste. Nothing is a waste. Faeces fertilise the earth, produce compost out of which vegetative life will grow. Crouching to defecate, or to give birth, goes with well-grounded feet, flexible legs and an open pelvis. We too will rot, blood and faeces, in order to create new life. That is another truth that is evaded and concealed at Argos, which therefore becomes a sterile regime.

To give meaning to loss, and to death, and institute disciplines which acknowledge and regulate our time-bounded existence, is the business of the Larissa funeral rites and games, which occur on neutral ground and in a context of present happening. This regulation can be enacted awarely in the lower bowel, where all the issues of integration and disintegration, and the muscular capacity to hold and let go, are part of the process of formation of faeces. The formation is never perfect: the 'accident' of the killing of Acrisius is like the toilet-training 'accident', which always has a meaning in its context. (The discus could symbolise faeces, the gust of wind farting: infantile means of 'anal attack' on authority.) The fault in the rigid systems is there to question their rigidity. Mistakes and failures are part of our learning to relate more flexibly to the body's realities.

New territory: the nature of balance in space

The removal to new ground by Perseus and Andromeda is the re-grounding, the landing on earth whose support one claims. This re-grounding undoes finally the painful body posture which maintains the Acrisius control – the pulling away from the ground, tensing of muscles to close the pelvic floor, holding the breath, stressing the lower back. The growth was perverted at the time of learning to walk, coinciding with toilet training. Whole body re-alignment helps to unweave this complex network of tensions: Perseus will institute appropriate games in his new domain.

The legs themselves, holding themselves up, will need to establish a new balance as they let their weight down to the earth through the feet. With the release of the sexual charge in the pelvis, the energy flows downward.

To the ungrounded legs, the issues of weakness and strength in mutual support were previously critical: the relationship between left and right leg usually reflects the feminine/masculine mother/father relationship. The tendency in Western society is a Danae/Polydectes–Acrisius relationship: the right leg is rigid, thrusting, pointing the direction, at the same time controlling the pelvic area, leading, overworked, not prepared to give over and allow strength to develop in the left leg. The left leg is weakened by under-use and the absence of positive energy, but less resistant and rigid, capable of taking the weight if need be but then easily exhausted by the burden, by the need to keep the pace set by the right. The left foot can be more tenacious to the ground, more in contact than the right foot, which is full of tensions, pulling away from the earth. This whole complex of the legs can be let go when earth is trusted as a support.

Perseus and Andromeda, right and left 'legs', safe on their own territory, releasing and channelling their sexuality, non-perfectionist about performance, breathing easily and unhurriedly, find the right balance and stability. And here they are not afraid to fall. Legs know they need to fall to the ground often as they learn how to build up their strength to walk on it. And in time they will take part in a wider rhythmic dance and celebrate life.

Breath, heart, lungs, pharynx: from the oracle to Gorgophone

When one is properly grounded and the energy allowed to flow through, as it is in Eastern meditation practice, in full orgasm, or in

179

a healthily regulated system, the spirit enters into the channel of the body (von Dürkheim 1956). The breath (Zeus-Prana-Ruach) comes through heart and lungs which are not chronically tensed, but can open and close appropriately. So the capacity for love, serenity, union with the universe, appreciation of beauty, is there, to be felt with awe. And at times to be closed against, for its power is very great, and we must also be able to contract when need be into our finite limited selves.

From the beginning of the myth the 'heart' of the story has been Danae, and she is still there at the end (as are so many widows of men who died of heart failure or in heartless wars). Danae's connection with the oracle's voiced wisdom, her heart-broken connection with her father, is another unspoken secret of Argos. The heart and voice were locked up. Inspiration, breath, from Zeus enabled them to avoid the total suffocation threatened by the rib-cage of her prison. The constriction of the sea-chest – the pharynx or throat, perhaps – prolonged the silence, breath held. And she continues to breathe painfully through all the suffering, pressure and conflict in Seriphos, while Perseus grows, her heart's need for reconciliation unmet. Her refuge in the temple with Dictys is a renewal of the spirit through meditation, breathing freely in a sanctuary with a heart companion. The release by Perseus of the pressure on her of Polydectes and Acrisius allow her to breathe more deeply in the open air of Larissa. But the games which show her how breathing may be regulated for creative purposes – as in sport, spoken poetry and music – are not for her: they are masculine mysteries and she remains silent, still holding her deep truth in her gut, which is not connected to Perseus's activity, the story woven and told by the active higher-pitched aspiring voices of the upper chest. Yet she, the 'still small voice' perhaps, is still there, still breathing in the background, the vital connection with the voice of the oracle and the inspiration of Zeus, watching the predicted drama unfold, the heart that beats throughout everything and survives if it keeps faith with its own modest potential and accepts the limitations of its one life. Her wisdom has been in silence, in saving her breath, and allowing her stronger son, and her daughter-in-law and grand-daughter, to do what she cannot do. She is not envious now: the envious Medusa is dead.

In individual body experience, when we are confident that we can always breathe, that our heart can survive the experiences of heartbreak, pressure, despair, weary exhaustion, pain, loss – as it had to in our birth – then we can re-connect to the deep gut knowledge of those experiences and throw them up, sing them out, call, protest. This is Andromeda. The channel of the windpipe and the pharynx opens: heart and voice and belly and sex are one. The deep passionate voice of the whole person, who is properly grounded, is in its total conviction, incontrovertible: courageous, life-affirming. Andromeda, in extremis, calls for care, salvation, healing and demands compassion for her passion: Perseus must answer. The silence of centuries is broken as women talk freely of menstruation, of sexual abuse and incestuous control, and voice their deeply felt 'No' at Greenham and elsewhere. When men listen, when in our bodies our ears and our masculine detachment and organising ability pay attention to what our whole body is asserting and needing, and respect that, then we can reach the simple confidence in fearless action of Gorgophone, who openly declares the spiritual wisdom of woman and the body and acts on her conviction. Her name means killer of the Gorgon, but it could doubtless also mean the voice of the Gorgon – that profound voice of the darkness of the womb and bowel that connects us to blood, to moon, and to earth.

Earth cannot be totally consumed by fire. If the pyre is the mixed rage and aspiration and self-destructiveness of our masculine controlled spirituality and sexuality – an overheated passion, an ill-tempered voice, then Gorgophone is the voice of a steadier, deeper spirit. Her clear voice speaks for the pulse of the blood, and the inner rhythms that connect us with time past and future, giving a meaning to life and its preservation on earth that goes far beyond one self-centred holocaust.

Chapter 13

Creative mythology:
The uses of myth in group settings

There is nothing new about the 'use' of myth. Dramatists, novelists, poets have always drawn on mythology for their work. Old truths find new meaning in the modern versions which are written or staged, and never fail in their powerful archetypal impact. Psychologists have always explored profound human themes through myth: the findings of anthropology illuminate their significance even further. One of the problems (which I have encountered in writing this book) is to concentrate and focus: it is easy to get lost in fascinating proliferations of ideas and associations. The use of dramatic exploration in group settings has proved an effective way of containing potentially unmanageable material – both imaginative and emotional – relative to themes which are for most participants highly charged. Within the limited time and space focusing is possible and considerable intensity achieved: the aim is to give an opportunity for the myth to be experienced in a variety of ways: it does its work at a conscious and unconscious level and reverberates long after.

The Perseus myth was used in the 'Absent Father' workshops, which had an avowed therapeutic aim and were attended predominantly by people who were or had been in transpersonal or humanistic therapy or analysis, or were accustomed to 'growth' work. I have also used myth in other settings, such as educational conferences, with people who had come together to address certain problems of common interest. Using a dynamic mode of exploring a relevant myth gives immediate stimulus and focus to issues which cannot be treated solely in a mental or theoretical way.

Workshops in creative mythology

The usual structure, which was developed by Jane Malcomson and myself, is of a weekend meeting, sometimes beginning with a Friday evening session, which helps establish group cohesion and adds a night to the experience: there are invariably relevant dreams, which tend to come on the second night. But we have conducted successful one-day and three-hour workshops also. Numbers of participants have ranged from six to twenty.

The aim is to offer the experience at several levels:

Fantasy-imaginative: expressed by group members in drawing, poetry, story-telling, etc.

Bodily: expressed in movement and mime.

Mental-theoretical: expressed through interpretation and discussion.

Poetic-associative: creative work by other artists, poets, musicians, etc. is incorporated.

Dramatic-inventive: improvisation of a modern version, or associated dynamic exploration, e.g. TV interviews with characters, invention of new myths, altered versions, rituals, etc.

As with all such groupwork there is an alternation between individual activity and group activity. Frequent feedback sessions, in small groups or in the large group, punctuate the weekend, so that there is a valuable sharing of reactions and ideas, which itself intensifies the power of the myth as an experience of collective creativity. Its location in the collective unconscious has proved indisputable: people have dreamed elements of the myth before the workshop without knowing what myth would be used for the theme chosen.

In a two-day workshop the first day gives the group the chance to become familiar with the myth and absorb its impact, and the second day is spent expanding and integrating the experience with the creative resources of those present.

A typical first day begins with 'warm-up' and 'inclusion' to allow the group to arrive comfortably and be present. After some consideration of people's concern with the stated theme of the workshop, the myth is introduced, told purely as a story, without comment. Then comes the movement work: in this each person identifies, alone, with each character at successive stages of the myth. There might also be work in twos or threes to experience a particular dynamic, *.*e.g. Acrisius locking up Danae; the Danae/Perseus/Polydectes triad. The movement is almost all non-verbal, mimed, with the emphasis on feeling the energy of the archetypal character or interaction in the body and feelings. Periodically there is a pause while group members write notes: impressions, poems, or draw what was experienced, and/or talk briefly in twos or threes about it. Some of the creative work will be directed to express what cannot be acted or mimed, e.g. a drawing of what Perseus sees in the mirror, a poem as if by Pegasus describing the feeling of flying.

After the whole myth has been gone through, the large group shares its experience in discussion with the leaders, relating it to events and experiences in their own lives: the leaders contribute whatever seems appropriate. Feelings can be powerfully aroused, and participants may need support in handling and expressing them. Interpersonal feelings and conflicts surface in the group also: they are reflected on in their relatedness to the theme and the myth, which is kept as the focus and containing structure for the group process.

When the myth is acted through on the second day – a modern version invented and improvised by the participants – its importance as a containing and facilitating medium becomes very clear. Myth is about movement and collective experience: it must take its course, inexorably, and cannot wait for individual resistance to what is being played out: group members have to experience the tenson between their personal myth and the myth that fate, the gods or the oracle have decreed. For instance, Perseus might feel he cannot bring himself to cut off the Medusa's head. The group leader who directs the drama holds the participants to the boundaries of time and of the given story: she becomes 'fate' itself (and is often not thanked for it!).

The improvisation is put together in the manner familiar to drama teachers: the group decide the modern setting and fill in the details, people choose their roles and plan individual scenes. The leader talks them into role, helps with setting the scenes, props, etc. At the end there is feedback in role, each person saying what they felt during the action. De-roling follows, and discussion as observers, with input also by leaders and anyone who was watching, not acting.

Further integration, depending on the time available, might include expanding or altering the myth, re-runs of emotionally unsatisfactory 'performances', individual creative work, writing the story, for instance, from an unusual viewpoint, such as Zeus's or Dictys's. Or the group might invent rituals relevant to their own needs, e.g. a ritual for divorce, a joint 'coronation' for Perseus and Andromeda, an alternative funeral for Gorgophone's husband. The day ends with a statement from each person about their experience of the whole workshop, and how their attitude may have changed from the viewpoint they arrived with.

The choice of a myth, and the way of handling it, is by no means simple, and many of the myths emerging from patriarchal cultures will stimulate impulses to challenge and re-write: these needs must be catered for. The Genesis creation story has many times provided a unique opportunity to explore one of the most all-pervasive complexes of the Western psyche, whose rooted strength is both denied and indisputable: in working with it, realising its psychological power, introducing revisions, following the process of Adam and Eve and their sons, there is opportunity for significant revaluation at all levels of experiencing. Other myths we have used included the Demeter/Persephone legend, in workshops exploring mother/daughter relationships, the Eros and Psyche story, and the Sumerian myth of Erishkegal and Inanna, both relevant to sisterhood, and to the dark and light faces of love.

In settings which are not specifically geared to personal therapeutic development the techniques will be similar but the emphasis different, dictated by the context and by how far those present are able and willing to take part in movement and drama. I have successfully worked with myth as follows:

In workshops on creativity, the Danae–Perseus myth, the Genesis story.
In conferences on gender, sexism, and on religion, the Genesis story.
At a conference on war, the story of Cain and Abel.
At a conference for English lecturers, mime and movement techniques were used to explore *Wuthering Heights* at a mythic level.

The story of Antigone was twice used as a simulation exercise at teachers' conference workshops. Translated to a setting in a comprehensive school and set up with the boundaries customary in simulations, it provided an excellent means of exploring issues of authority and loyalty.

I hope interested readers will feel encouraged to experiment with the dynamic use of myth in whatever setting they work in. Some experience of drama or psychodrama and familiarity with simulation procedures is necessary. Most important is that clear boundaries be marked to cater for the leader's (in)experience and capacity to handle and channel the feelings aroused. We work most effectively at the level we are comfortable with. However, it is inevitable that we may be led into deeper waters. When the discomfort at the boundary becomes acute it is time to review and perhaps re-set the boundary. I trust that Perseus's experiences will offer guidance at that point.

Notes

Chapter 1

1 Roland Barthes, in *Mythologies*.
2 Arthur Miller's play *A View from the Bridge* offers a powerful example of this dynamic.
3 This whole area is explored by Maureen Green (1976). *Goodbye Father* provides an excellent psycho-sociological survey of current developments. But the subject is still not much aired: her book is out of print, and twelve years on we have a heightened urgency and a greater need to see the dangerous implications of what is happening.
4 'The Parable of the Old Man and the Young' (Owen, *Collected Poems*).
5 A recent and very relevant version of this archetypal drama is John le Carré's novel *The Little Drummer Girl* (le Carré 1983).

Chapter 2

1 For an excellent discussion of the status of gods and myths, see Liz Greene (1985) in particular the introduction. Her reading of the Perseus myth (pp. 228–31) is very interesting.
2 Sophia, goddess of wisdom, 'came to a high mountain and spent time seated there, so that she desired herself alone . . . She fulfilled her desire and became pregnant from her desire.' From Elaine Pagéls's *The Gnostic Gospels*, quoted by Asphodel (1987).
3 Woodman (1985). Chapter 4, especially pp. 80–1, looks at the deeper symbolism of the Virgin Mary.
4 Anne Dickson (1985) writes from long experience of working with women's sexuality and offers an unvarnished picture of how it is experienced, and capable of change.
5 See Stanley Keleman (1975a, 1982). The more recent book looks at the

complexities and consequences of 'sexual liberation' with a rare profundity and spiritual concern.

Chapter 3

1 For a summary of recent findings see Pirani (1978). Grof (1975), Lake (1987), Janov (1973), Feher (1980), Laing (1976) write of regression experiences. Fodor (1949) and Mott (1959) deduced much from dream-analysis.
2 Sheehy (1976) gives a useful introduction to the nature of life-transitions. Gordon (1978) explores extensively the anthropological and psychological implications of the 'death-experience' for creativity.

Chapter 4

1 Arcana (1983); Green (1976).
2 For valuable discussions of parental roles in family life, see Robin Skynner *One Flesh, Separate Persons* (London, Constable, 1976), and Robin Skynner and John Cleese *Families and how to survive them* (Methuen, London, 1983).
3 *Alternatives* by John Osmond and Angela Graham (Thorsons, 1984), describes this development in its first chapter 'The Alternative Movement'.
4 Quotation from Audre Lorde, 'Manchild. A Black Lesbian Feminist's Response' in *Conditions*, 4, 1979.
5 Irene Claremont de Castillejo (1973) has an excellent chapter on 'Woman as Mediator'.
6 Thomas (1984). He is making the important point that sex may be seen as a game, not as a serious power-struggle: the same idea can apply to politics.
7 'The Boss', a short story by Dan Jacobson, gives a striking account of such a negotiation, and how a Medusa-figure gets caught in it (Jacobson 1971).
8 *Biographia Literaria*, 1816.

Chapter 5

1 *The Wise Wound* (Shuttle and Redgrove 1986) explores extensively the power and status of menstruation. For interesting references to the Medusa, see pp. 78 and 247–9.
2 Segal (1979) quotes this in the chapter 'Envy and Gratitude' p. 143.
3 Poem by Nancy Brinton.
4 Woodman (1982), from the Preface.
5 An interesting case is that of Queenie Leavis, wife of the literary critic F. R. Leavis, who after his death revealed some unsuspected facts about

their lifelong working partnership; she already had a Medusa reputation.

6 See Shuttle and Redgrove (1986), chapter VI.
7 See Introduction to *Deborah*, by Esther Kreitman (London, Virago, 1983).
8 See Ackroyd (1985).
9 The whole remarkable story can be read (in French) in *Camille Claudel* by Reine-Marie Paris (Editions Gallimard, 1984). Bernard Howells contributes an interesting piece on the mirror-shield of Perseus and the mutually reflective nature of Camille's relationship with Paul.
10 Nicholas Humphrey, 'Four Minutes to Midnight' Bronowski Memorial Lecture 1981, reprinted in *The Listener*, 29 Oct 1981.
11 Maurice Friedman, *The Hidden Human Image*, o.p.

Chapter 6

1 The term was coined by Hanna Segal and is discussed in Gordon (1978). David Bakan, in *The Duality of Human Existence* (Beacon Press, 1966), describes the same phenomenon as 'idolatry'.
2 Op. cit. Chapter 1.
3 The difference between patriarchal and matriarchal myths of martyrdom is relevant here. See the discussion of this by Sylvia Brinton Perera in *Descent to the Goddess* (1981) pp. 20–1. The woman whose fantasy is described here did know of the Erishkegal-Inanna myth which is the subject of Perera's book. Rosemary Radford Ruether (1983) relates this to problems in Christian belief, ch. 10.
4 This double-bind is well described in Helen Franks's excellent book on this stage of life, *Prime Time* (Fontana, 1981) pp. 181ff. Shuttle and Redgrove (1986) refer to it as the howlback effect.
5 Quoted by Ruether (1983), pp. 171–2.
6 Ruether (1983), describes and in her book effects the process of discarding the concept – misconcept – of a patriarchal God and its hold on us. See also Mary Daly, *Beyond God the Father* (1973).
7 See Nancy Friday, *My Mother, My Self* (Fontana/Collins, 1977). Also Sylvia Brinton Perera (1981), Introduction and ch. 1.
8 Natalie Rogers in *Emerging Woman* (Personal Press, 1980), a powerful document, describes her transition to wholly new ways of relating to others.
9 See Shuttle and Redgrove (1986), pp. 65–6.
10 Gail Sheehy looks usefully at this and other life transitions in *Passages* (1976) esp. pp. 456–64. See also Stein (1983) particularly for the male experience.

Chapter 7

1 Addiction to 'mindblowing' drugs like alcohol often masks the need for

genuine transcendence. This was found by Grof and Halifax in their work with the dying. See *The Human Encounter with Death* (London, Souvenir Press, 1978), pp. 214–15.

2 For a general introduction to this area – the paradigm shift, the quantum leap, brain development and its relation to creativity and evolution, see Ferguson (1982).

3 Quoted in *The Wise Wound* (Shuttle and Redgrove, 1986).

4 See *The Tao of Physics* by Fritjof Capra (Fontana, 1976).

5 Ken Wilber, in his exploration of the spectrum of personal-transpersonal psychology, names a 'Centaur' phase which relates to the Pegasus paradox in an interesting way (Wilber 1979).

Chapter 8

1 For illuminating work on relationships deriving from Jung's approach, see de Castillejo (1973), Greene (1977), and Woodman (1985), ch. 6. Keleman (1975a, 1982) from another perspective, offers many valuable insights.

2 'Eco-feminism' sees the close relationship between men's treatment of the earth and of women, and believes that change must occur in parallel. See *Reclaim the Earth*, ed. Caldecott and Leland (Women's Press, 1983). Also my poem and essay 'The Song of Songs for 1984' in *Glancing Fires* (Saunders 1987).

3 Britain is in danger of being put naked on the rock, exposed to the economic, military and social disaster that far larger, more powerful, belligerent nations and the monsters they spawn could unleash on her, if they decide to give Cassiopeia her come-uppance.

4 See Raphael Patai, *The Hebrew Goddess* (New York, Ktav Pubs, 1967).

5 For revealing comments on the status of the 'princess', and its social and physiological implications, see Mindell (1984) pp. 121–3. This is Cassiopeia: Andromeda matures perforce beyond this.

6 See Rowan 1987.

7 For an exploration of this polarity, see Lake (1986). I relate it to literary healing in 'The Song of Songs for 1984' (Saunders 1987).

8 Dickson (1985) exposes the power over women of that negative self-image, ch. 4.

9 Dan Jacobson's story 'The Little Pet' focuses poignantly on a middle-class family whose values are blown apart by this 'unacceptable face' of animal nature (Jacobson 1971).

10 For an account of invaluable work being done in this area of despair, see Macy (1983). Rowe (1985) also helps look at the threat, with 'unashamed' directness.

11 Perera (1986) explores the role and psychology of the scapegoat; she quotes a Sufi story which has interesting parallels with Andromeda's.

12 See Gordon (1978) for an examination of ego-boundaries in relation to

primitive African and more 'civilised' social organisation. Also relevant: von Durkheim (1956) and Wilber (1979).

13 The power of Africa, and the white man's relationship with Africa, is conveyed passionately in the writing of Laurens van der Post: his account of Jung's experience in Africa is relevant here (van der Post 1976).

Chapter 9

1 The Royal Family is afforded respect, protection, immunity not given to political leaders, which provides the needed 'sanctuary' in which the drama can happen and an 'ideal model' of family life be shaped. This is a wholly healthy area for 'play' and for the public exploration of many vital issues of family, authority, religion, power. The present British Royal Family's history has its parallels with our myth, and the matriarchal/patriarchal elements are worth pondering on. Prince Charles has undoubted Perseus qualities and origins, ambivalent fathering – Philip? Earl Mountbatten? Laurens van der Post? – a considerable consciousness of the spiritual significance of his role as dispossessed royalty and a determination to deal with the Medusa aspects of the orthodox medical and architectural worlds and other rigidified establishments. Diana has, like Andromeda, survived both personal family betrayal and the seductions of princess-hood, and retained her strength of commitment to the helpless innocent child both within and outside her. The roles of Danae and Medusa have been carried to some extent by the Queen and also by her sister Margaret. When we look back over the twentieth century we may well realise that Queen Elizabeth, from what may have seemed a very passive position, exerted a powerful and mostly benign matriarchal influence. At the same time there is the symbolic power of the Church, and the present Archbishop of Canterbury and his wife have become an influential partnership in the public imagination. Events in the Temple and the Palace are as significant symbolically in Britain today as they were in legendary Seriphos.

2 The American presidency, in the 1970s and 1980s, has manifested similar Acrisius characteristics, the White House becoming very like Argos at this stage of the myth.

3 Raymond Williams's novel *Border Country* is a particularly moving example of this confrontation between father and son. Barry Hines in his novel *The Blinder* explores this in the setting of the corrupt male world of football. Poets Tony Harrison, Geoffrey Hill and D. M. Thomas also are drawn to look at their working-class fathering.

4 The appalling violence and loss of life at the international football match in Brussels in May 1985 was sensitively interpreted by David Miller, sports correspondent of the London *Times*, whose comments (1 June 1985) show a rare understanding of the symbolic status of sport.

5 For a wise older woman's wisdom on this subject, see de Castillejo (1973). Also worth attention: *Look Me in the Eye* by Macdonald and Rich (London, Women's Press, 1984).

6 Relegated to the Apocrypha, *The Wisdom of Solomon* (chs 7–11) acknowledges the existence of feminine wisdom, a goddess-figure, who was there before God. She is acknowledged in Proverbs, ch. 8. See Asphodel (1987) and Woodman (1985).

Chapter 10

1 Poem by John Kirti Wheway.

Chapter 11

1 Ehrenzweig (1967) develops this concept in his inimitable brilliant way, particularly in relation to visual and plastic art. Milner (1950) had already shown its truth in her book, which itself manifests the creative process she is examining.

2 D. H. Lawrence went from the time-orientated *The Rainbow* to the space-orientated *Women in Love*. The First World War, for so many the confrontation with the Medusa, began after *The Rainbow* was finished.

3 For further exploration of these two modes, see Pirani (1979). Depth psychology, Freudian and Kleinian analysis, primal and other regression therapies, belong with the first kind of creativity: 'here-and-now' therapies such as Gestalt, psychosynthesis, bio-energetics, behavioural psychology, belong with the second. Wilber (1979) has a not dissimilar way of seeing the different psychologies and therapies.

4 Among the Kleinians: Milner (1950), Ehrenzweig (1967) and Winnicott (1971). Of the Jungians: the work of Ira Progoff, James Hillman, Rosemary Gordon and Marion Woodman (1985). James Vargiu, among others, working within the framework of psychosynthesis, has made valuable contributions to the study of creativity.

5 See *Gestalt Therapy Now* (Penguin) and Perls, Hefferline and Goodman (1973).

6 See 'Rebirth – the Quintessential Creative Process' in Pirani (1978). Also David Wasdell, *The Primal Matrix of Social Process* (London, Urchin, 1987) and Feher (1980), ch. 3.

7 See Barbara Black Koltuv, *The Book of Lilith* (Maine, Nicolas Hayes, 1986), p. 116. Also Shuttle and Redgrove (1986), pp. 81 and 84. And the first poem below, p. 150.

8 See *In Dora's Case: Freud: Hysteria: Feminism*, ed. Bernheimer and Kahane (London, Virago, 1985). See also Suttie (1935) for early perceptive criticisms of Freud.

9 The classic literary example is of Iago and Othello. The Salieri–Mozart relationship as portrayed in Schaffer's play *Amadeus* is

another. For a hilarious portrayal of the excesses of envy, see Howard Jacobson's novel *Coming from Behind* (1983), Black Swan edition, pp. 22–3.

10 Melanie Klein, 'Some Theoretical Conclusions Regarding the Emotional Life of the Infant', *Envy and Gratitude* (London, Hogarth Press, 1975).

11 D.H. Lawrence went into exile, geographically. T. S. Eliot went into exile emotionally.

12 An interesting discovery made by Rosemary Gordon about this stage of the Perseus myth exemplifies the transition in action (Gordon 1985).

13 See Ackroyd (1985) and my (unpublished) essay 'T. S. Eliot and 20th century consciousness.'

14 Quoted in *Proms 87* (BBC Books, 1987), p. 37.

Chapter 12

1 See Fodor (1949), Mott (1959), Mindell (1984, 1985) and Shuttle and Redgrove (1986). It is quite common for people to dream pre-cognitively of their own dying – usually symbolically – even if they do not know consciously of the impending death.

2 The work of Carl and Stephanie Simonton with cancer sufferers has successfully included visualisation. Biofeedback practices are described by Barbara Brown in *New Mind, New Body: Biofeedback* (London, Hodder & Stoughton, 1975).

3 The best Western approaches to the body's creativity are those of the neo-Reichian bio-eneregeticists: Kelley, Pierrakos, Boyeson, Lowen and Kaleman. See also the work of David Boadella, mostly published in the journal *Energy and Character*.

4 In an article in *Energy and Character*, vol. 10, no. 3.

5 Dentistry has been curing migraine by operating to release tension in the jaw.

6 The pianist Paul Crossley described this in a TV programme, February 1987. The concerto was written for Paul Wittgenstein (who lost his right arm in the war) and became Ravel's attempt to come to terms with a profound disturbance of the feminine and masculine. Ravel never married, and was devoted to his mother. The war shattered the idyllic European world they inhabited, and she died at the same time. He could not handle this Medusa situation and the split in himself. Crossley sees the concerto as a work of disintegration, an unhealed wound, the left hand in painful relationship with an almost ruthless orchestra. Ravel subsequently died after a long illness of mental debilitation.

7 See chapter 4 of *The Wise Wound*, especially pp. 136ff.

Selected bibliography

Ackroyd, Peter (1985), *T. S. Eliot*, London, Abacus Books.

Arcana, Judith (1983), *Every Mother's Son*, London, Women's Press/N.Y., Anchor Press.

Asphodel (1987), 'Goddesses of Wisdom', *Arachne*, no. 6.

Bateson, Gregory (1973), *Steps to an Ecology of Mind*, London, Paladin Books.

Bradley, Marion (1984), *The Mists of Avalon*, London, Sphere Books.

Chernin, Kim (1985), *In My Mother's House*, London, Virago Press.

Daly, Mary (1973), *Beyond God the Father*, Boston, Beacon Press.

de Castillejo, Irene Claremont (1973), *Knowing Woman*, New York, Harper Colophon.

Dickson, Anne (1985), *The Mirror Within*, London, Quartet Books.

Ehrenzweig, Anton (1967), *The Hidden Order of Art*, Berkeley, University of California Press.

Eliot, T. S. (1920), *The Sacred Wood*, London.

Eliot, T. S. (1969), *The Complete Poems and Plays*, London, Faber.

Erikson, Erik (1958), *Young Man Luther*, New York, W. W. Norton.

Erikson, Erik (1965), *Childhood and Society*, London, Penguin Books.

Erikson, Erik (1978), *Toys and Reasons*, London, Marion Boyars.

Feher, Elizabeth (1980), *The Psychology of Birth*, London, Souvenir Books.

Ferguson, Marilyn (1982), *The Aquarian Conspiracy*, London, Paladin Books.

Fodor, Nandor (1949), *The Search for the Beloved*, Hermitage Press.

Franks, Helen (1981), *Prime Time*, London, Pan Books.

Gendlin, Eugene (1981), *Focusing*, New York, Bantam Books.

Gordon, Rosemary (1978), *Dying and Creating: A Search for Meaning*, London, Society of Analytical Psychology.

Gordon, Rosemary (1985), 'Losing and Finding: The Location of Archetypal Experience', *Journal of Analytical Psychology*, vol. 30, pp. 117–33.

Graves, Robert (1955), *The Greek Myths*, London, Penguin Books.

Green, Maureen (1976), *Goodbye Father*, London, Routledge & Kegan Paul.

Greene, Liz (1977), *Relating*, London, Coventure.

Greene, Liz (1985), *The Astrology of Fate*, London, Unwin.

Grof, Stanislav (1975), *Realms of the Human Unconscious*, New York, Viking Press.

Harrison, John (1986), *Love Your Disease. It's keeping you healthy*, London, Angus & Robertson.

Hillman, James (1964), 'Betrayal' in *Loose Ends*, Dallas, Spring Pubs, 1975.

Hillman, James (1973), 'The Great Mother, Her Son, Her Hero, and the Puer' in *Fathers and Mothers*, ed. P. Berry, Dallas, Spring Pubs.

Hillman, James (1976), *Suicide and the Soul*, Dallas, Spring Pubs.

Hillman, James (1978), *The Myth of Analysis*, New York, Harper & Row.

Hillman, James (1983), *Healing Fiction*, New York, Station Hill Press.

I Ching (1983), trans by R. Wilhelm, London, Routledge & Kegan Paul.

Jacobson, Dan (1971), *A Way of Life and other stories*, London, Longmans Imprint Series.

Janov, Arthur (1973), *The Feeling Child*, New York, Simon & Schuster.

Keleman, Stanley (1975a), *The Human Ground: Sexuality, Self and Survival*, Palo Alto, Science & Behavior Books.

Keleman, Stanley (1975b), *Your Body Speaks its Mind*, New York, Simon & Schuster.

Keleman, Stanley (1982), *In Defense of Heterosexuality*, Berkeley, Center Press.

Laing, R. D. (1976), *The Facts of Life*, London, Allen Lane.

Lake, Frank (1986), *Clinical Theology*, new abridged ed., London, Darton Longman & Todd.

Lake, Frank (1987), *Tight Corners in Pastoral Counselling*, London, Darton Longman & Todd.

Leboyer, Frédéric (1975), *Birth Without Violence*, London, Wildwood House.

le Carré, John (1983), *The Little Drummer Girl*, London, Pan Books.

le Carré, John (1986), *The Perfect Spy*, London, Pan Books.

Macy, Joanna Rogers (1983), *Despair and Personal Power in the Nuclear Age*, Philadelphia, New Society Publishers.

Milner, Marion (1950), *On Not Being Able to Paint*, London, Heinemann Educational [2nd edn 1977].

Mindell, Arnold (1984), *Dreambody*, London, Routledge & Kegan Paul.

Mindell, Arnold (1985), *Working with the Dreaming Body*, London, Routledge & Kegan Paul.

Mott, Francis (1959), *The Nature of the Self*, London and New York, Integration Publishing Co.

Owen, Wilfred, (1967), *Collected Poems*, London, Chatto & Windus.

Perera, Sylvia Brinton (1981), *Descent to the Goddess: A way of initiation for women*, Toronto, Inner City Books.

Selected bibliography

Perera, Sylvia Brinton (1986), *The Scapegoat Complex: Shadow and Guilt*, Toronto, Inner City Books.

Perls, Fritz (1969) [1946], *Ego, Hunger and Aggression*, New York, Vintage Books.

Perls, Fritz, Hefferline, Ralph and Goodman, Paul (1973) [1951], *Gestalt Therapy*, London, Penguin Books.

Pirani, Alix (1978) (ed.), *Birth and Rebirth*, London, Self and Society.

Pirani, Alix (1979), 'Rebirth Creativity and Orgastic Creativity', *Energy and Character*, vol. 10, no. 1.

Reich, Wilhelm (1972) [1942], *The Function of the Orgasm*, London, Panther Books.

Roberts, Michele (1984), *The Wild Girl*, London, Methuen.

Rowan, John (1987), *The Horned God*, London, Routledge & Kegan Paul.

Rowe, Dorothy (1983), *Depression*, London, Routledge & Kegan Paul.

Rowe, Dorothy (1985), *Living with the Bomb*, London, Routledge & Kegan Paul.

Ruether, Rosemary Radford (1983), *Sexism and God-Talk*, London, SCM Press.

Saunders, Lesley (1987) (ed.), *Glancing Fires*, London, Women's Press.

Segal, Hanna (1979), *Klein*, London, Fontana Books.

Sheehy, Gail (1976), *Passages*, London, Corgi Books.

Shuttle, Penelope and Redgrove, Peter (1986), *The Wise Wound*, London, Paladin Books.

Starhawk (1979), *The Spiral Dance*, San Francisco, Harper & Row.

Stein, Murray (1983), *In Midlife*, Dallas, Spring Pubs.

Suttie, Ian (1935), *The Origins of Love and Hate*, London, Routledge & Kegan Paul.

Thomas, D. M. (1981), *The White Hotel*, London, Penguin Books.

Thomas, D. M. (1984), 'You're too hot to handle', *Cosmopolitan*, March 1984.

van der Post, Laurens (1976), *Jung and the Story of Our Time*, London, Hogarth Press.

von Dürkheim, Karlfried (1956), *Hara*, London, Mandala Books.

Wilber, Ken (1979), *No Boundary*, Los Angeles, Center Publications.

Winnicott, D. W. (1971), *Playing and Reality*, London, Tavistock and Penguin Books.

Woodman, Marion (1980), *The Owl was a Baker's Daughter*, Toronto, Inner City Books.

Woodman, Marion (1982), *Addiction to Perfection*, Toronto, Inner City Books.

Woodman, Marion (1985), *The Pregnant Virgin*, Toronto, Inner City Books.

Index

ARKANA – NEW-AGE BOOKS FOR MIND, BODY AND SPIRIT

With over 150 titles currently in print, Arkana is the leading name in quality new-age books for mind, body and spirit. Arkana encompasses the spirituality of both East and West, ancient and new, in fiction and non-fiction. A vast range of interests are covered, including Psychology and Transformation, Health, Science and Mysticism, Women's Spirituality and Astrology.

If you would like a catalogue of Arkana books, please write to:

Arkana Marketing Department
Penguin Books Ltd
27 Wright's Lane
London W8 5TZ

ARKANA – NEW-AGE BOOKS FOR MIND, BODY AND SPIRIT

A selection of titles already published or in preparation

The Networking Book: People Connecting with People
Jessica Lipnack and Jeffrey Stamps

Networking – forming human connections to link ideas and resources – is the natural form of organization for an era based on information technology. Principally concerned with those networks whose goal is a peaceful yet dynamic future for the world, *The Networking Book* – written by two world-famous experts – profiles hundreds of such organizations worldwide, operating at every level from global tele-communications to word of mouth.

Chinese Massage Therapy: A Handbook of Therapeutic Massage Compiled at the Anhui Medical School Hospital, China
Translated by Hor Ming Lee and Gregory Whincup

There is a growing movement among medical practitioners in China today to mine the treasures of traditional Chinese medicine – acupuncture, herbal medicine and massage therapy. Directly translated from a manual in use in Chinese hospitals, *Chinese Massage Therapy* offers a fresh understanding of this time-tested medical alternative.

Dialogues with Scientists and Sages: The Search for Unity
Renée Weber

In their own words, contemporary scientists and mystics – from the Dalai Lama to Stephen Hawking – share with us their richly diverse views on space, time, matter, energy, life, consciousness, creation and our place in the scheme of things. Through the immediacy of verbatim dialogue, we encounter scientists who endorse mysticism, and those who oppose it; mystics who dismiss science, and those who embrace it.

Zen and the Art of Calligraphy
Omōri Sōgen and Terayama Katsujo

Exploring every element of the relationship between Zen thought and the artistic expression of calligraphy, two long-time practitioners of Zen, calligraphy and swordsmanship show how Zen training provides a proper balance of body and mind, enabling the calligrapher to write more profoundly, freed from distraction or hesitation.

ARKANA – NEW-AGE BOOKS FOR MIND, BODY AND SPIRIT

A selection of titles already published or in preparation

Judo – The Gentle Way Alan Fromm and Nicolas Soames

Like many of the martial arts, Judo primarily originated not as a method of self-defence but as a system for self-development. This book reclaims the basic principles underlying the technique, re-emphasizing Judo as art rather than sport.

Women of Wisdom Tsultrim Allione

By gathering together the rich and vivid biographies of six Tibetan female mystics, and describing her own experiences of life as a Tibetan Buddhist nun and subsequently as a wife and mother, Tsultrim Allione tells the inspirational stories of women who have overcome every difficulty to attain enlightenment and liberation.

Natural Healers' Acupressure Handbook
Volume II: Advanced G-Jo Michael Blate

Volume I of this bestselling handbook taught the basic G-Jo – or acupressure – techniques, used to bring immediate relief to hundreds of symptoms. In Volume II Michael Blate teaches us to find and heal our own 'root organs' – the malfunctioning organs that are the true roots of disease and suffering – in order to restore balance and, with it, health and emotional contentment.

Shape Shifters: Shaman Women in Contemporary Society
Michele Jamal

Shape Shifters profiles 14 shaman women of today – women who, like the shamans of old, have passed through an initiatory crisis and emerged as spiritual leaders empowered to heal the pain of others.

'The shamanic women articulate what is intuitively felt by many "ordinary" women. I think this book has the potential to truly "change a life"' – Dr Jean Shinoda Bolen, author of *Goddesses in Everywoman*.

ARKANA – NEW-AGE BOOKS FOR MIND, BODY AND SPIRIT

A selection of titles already published or in preparation

The Ghost in the Machine Arthur Koestler

Koestler's classic work – which can be read alone or as the conclusion of his trilogy on the human mind – is concerned not with human creativity but with human pathology.

'He has seldom been as impressive, as scientifically far-ranging, as lively-minded or as alarming as on the present occasion' – John Raymond in the *Financial Times*.

T'ai Chi Ch'uan and Meditation Da Liu

Today T'ai Chi Ch'uan is known primarily as a martial art – but it was originally developed as a complement to meditation. Both disciplines involve alignment of the self with the Tao, the ultimate reality of the universe. Da Liu shows how to combine T'ai Chi Ch'uan and meditation, balancing the physical and spiritual aspects to attain good health and harmony with the universe.

Return of the Goddess Edward C. Whitmont

Amidst social upheaval and the questioning of traditional gender roles, a new myth is arising: the myth of the ancient Goddess who once ruled earth and heaven before the advent of patriarchy and patriachal religion. Here one of the world's leading Jungian analysts argues that our society, long dominated by male concepts of power and aggression, is today experiencing a resurgence of the feminine.

The Strange Life of Ivan Osokin P. D. Ouspensky

If you had the chance to live your life again, what would you do with it? Ouspensky's novel, set in Moscow, on a country estate and in Paris, tells what happens to Ivan Ososkin when he is sent back twelve years to his stormy schooldays, early manhood and early loves. First published in 1947, the *Manchester Guardian* praised it as 'a brilliant fantasy . . . written to illustrate the theme that we do not live life but that life lives us'.

ARKANA – NEW-AGE BOOKS FOR MIND, BODY AND SPIRIT

A selection of titles already published or in preparation

Head Off Stress: Beyond the Bottom Line D. E. Harding

Learning to head off stress takes no time at all and is impossible to forget – all it requires is that we dare take a fresh look at ourselves. This infallible and revolutionary guide from the author of *On Having No Head* – whose work C. S. Lewis described as 'highest genius' – shows how.

Shiatzu: Japanese Finger Pressure for Energy, Sexual Vitality and Relief from Tension and Pain
Yukiko Irwin with James Wagenvoord

The product of 4000 years of Oriental medicine and philosophy, Shiatzu is a Japanese variant of the Chinese practice of acupuncture. Fingers, thumbs and palms are applied to the 657 pressure points that the Chinese penetrate with gold and silver needles, aiming to maintain health, increase vitality and promote well-being.

The Magus of Strovolos: The Extraordinary World of a Spiritual Healer Kyriacos C. Markides

This vivid account introduces us to the rich and intricate world of Daskalos, the Magus of Strovolos – a true healer who draws upon a seemingly limitless mixture of esoteric teachings, psychology, reincarnation, demonology, cosmology and mysticism, from both East and West.

'This is a really marvellous book . . . one of the most extraordinary accounts of a "magical" personality since Ouspensky's account of Gurdjieff' – Colin Wilson

Meetings With Remarkable Men G. I. Gurdjieff

All that we know of the early life of Gurdjieff – one of the great spiritual masters of this century – is contained within these colourful and profound tales of adventure. The men who influenced his formative years had no claim to fame in the conventional sense; what made them remarkable was the consuming desire they all shared to understand the deepest mysteries of life.

ARKANA – NEW-AGE BOOKS FOR MIND, BODY AND SPIRIT

A selection of titles already published or in preparation

The TM Technique Peter Russell

Through a process precisely opposite to that by which the body accumulates stress and tension, transcendental meditation works to produce a state of profound rest, with positive benefits for health, clarity of mind, creativity and personal stability. Peter Russell's book has become the key work for everyone requiring a complete mastery of TM.

The Development of the Personality: Seminars in Psychological Astrology Volume I Liz Greene and Howard Sasportas

Taking as a starting point their groundbreaking work on the cross-fertilization between astrology and psychology, Liz Greene and Howard Sasportas show how depth psychology works with the natal chart to illuminate the experiences and problems all of us encounter throughout the development of our individual identity, from childhood onwards.

Homage to the Sun: The Wisdom of the Magus of Strovolos Kyriacos C. Markides

Homage to the Sun continues the adventure into the mysterious and extraordinary world of the spiritual teacher and healer Daskalos, the 'Magus of Strovolos'. The logical foundations of Daskalos' world of other dimensions are revealed to us – invisible masters, past-life memories and guardian angels, all explained by the Magus with great lucidity and scientific precision.

The Year I: Global Process Work Arnold Mindell

As we approach the end of the 20th century, we are on the verge of planetary extinction. Solving the planet's problems is literally a matter of life and death. Arnold Mindell shows how his famous and groundbreaking process-orientated psychology can be extended so that our own sense of global awareness can be developed and we – the whole community of earth's inhabitants – can comprehend the problems and work together towards solving them.

ARKANA – NEW-AGE BOOKS FOR MIND, BODY AND SPIRIT

A selection of titles already published or in preparation

Being Intimate: A Guide to Successful Relationships
John and Kris Amodeo

This invaluable guide aims to enrich one of the most important – yet often problematic – aspects of our lives: intimate relationships and friendships.

'A clear and practical guide to the realization and communication of authentic feelings, and thus an excellent pathway towards lasting intimacy and love' – George Leonard

The Brain Book Peter Russell

The essential handbook for brain users.

'A fascinating book – for everyone who is able to appreciate the human brain, which, as Russell says, is the most complex and most powerful information processor known to man. It is especially relevant for those who are called upon to read a great deal when time is limited, or who attend lectures or seminars and need to take notes' – *Nursing Times*

The Act of Creation Arthur Koestler

This second book in Koestler's classic trio of works on the human mind (which opened with *The Sleepwalkers* and concludes with *The Ghost in the Machine*) advances the theory that all creative activities – the conscious and unconscious processes underlying artistic originality, scientific discovery and comic inspiration – share a basic pattern, which Koestler expounds and explores with all his usual clarity and brilliance.

A Psychology With a Soul: Psychosynthesis in Evolutionary Context Jean Hardy

Psychosynthesis was developed between 1910 and the 1950s by Roberto Assagioli – an Italian psychiatrist who, like Jung, diverged from Freud in search of a more spiritually based understanding of human nature. Jean Hardy's account of this comprehensive approach to self-realization will be of great value to everyone concerned with personal integration and spiritual growth.